FAIRWAYS AND DREAMS

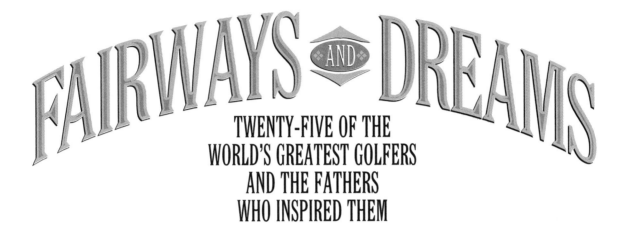

FAIRWAYS AND DREAMS

TWENTY-FIVE OF THE WORLD'S GREATEST GOLFERS AND THE FATHERS WHO INSPIRED THEM

MICHAEL ARKUSH

foreword by **Billy Casper**

RUTLEDGE HILL PRESS®

Nashville, Tennessee

Published in Nashville, Tennessee, by Rutledge Hill Press®, 211 Seventh Avenue North, Nashville, Tennessee 37219.

Distributed in Canada by H. B. Fenn & Company, Ltd., 34 Nixon Road, Bolton, Ontario L7E 1W2.

Distributed in Australia by The Five Mile Press Pty., Ltd., 22 Summit Road, Noble Park, Victoria 3174.

Distributed in New Zealand by Tandem Press, 2 Rugby Road, Birkenhead, Auckland 10.

Distributed in the United Kingdom by Verulam Publishing, Ltd., 152a Park Street Lane, Park Street, St. Albans, Hertfordshire AL2 2AU.

Typography by Compass Communications, Inc., Nashville, TN

Library of Congress Cataloging-in-Publication Data

Arkush, Michael.
    Fairways and dreams : twenty-five of the world's greatest golfers and the fathers who inspired them / Michael Arkush ; foreword by Billy Casper.
        p.   cm.
    ISBN 1-55853-597-7 (hardbound)
    1. Golfers—Biography.   2. Father and child.   I. Title.
    GV964.A1A75   1998   98-11090
                                                                                                                    CIP

Printed in the United States of America

1 2 3 4 5 6 7 8 9—01 00 99 98

To three women who have traveled my fairways and inspired my dreams:

My mom, Celia; my wife, Pauletta; and my daughter, Jade.

CONTENTS

FOREWORD

My upstairs den is packed with photographs. Each one, in its own unique way, is special, freezing a moment in my golf career I will never forget. Winged Foot, Olympic, Augusta—they all mean so much to me. So, of course, do the players who faced me and the fans who followed me. We were all partners in the same, often heroic, often harrowing, adventure we never wanted to abandon.

Nonetheless, as much as I value these photos, they are not the most important ones in my house. I have another collection, and this one does not show famous faces or famous golf courses. As a matter of fact, this one has very little to do with golf … and everything to do with life. This one shows my family.

It's a pretty big one. My wife, Shirley, and I have eleven children, six of whom we adopted.

They are, without question, our proudest achievement. It has not been an easy challenge; parenthood never is. But it has been a remarkable one, and I wouldn't exchange it for all the green jackets in Georgia. Winning a major could never compare to watching a son or daughter grow into the person you always knew they could become.

The golfers who tell their stories in this book are most fortunate. Each child requires the proper nurturing in those important early years, and they got it. Their fathers knew exactly when to criticize and when to encourage, when to supervise, and when to let go. No wonder they became the best in their business.

But their journey of discovery has only just begun. In the years ahead, quite a few of them will see their own kids leave the womb and enter the world, bolstered by the values and sensibilities they picked up at home. Will there be pitfalls? You bet. Will they second-guess themselves? Absolutely. Will some relationships with their kids be better than others? Sadly, yes.

Ultimately, though, they will take pride in a job well done. They will look at the pictures in their dens and realize, like I do, that what they did with their children was more valuable than anything they did with their careers. No amount of success can compensate for failure in the home.

—Billy Casper

ACKNOWLEDGMENTS

This book was far from a solo effort. First, I owe a tremendous debt to the golfers who agreed to contibute. By sharing such personal reflections, they revealed a side of themselves often hidden from the newspapers and microphones.

Like the golfers I interviewed, I needed a caddie to steer me in the right direction, to help me avoid the inherent pitfalls. Mike Towle, Rutledge Hill Press's executive editor, served that purpose, never losing focus. Our conversations always renewed my enthusiasm.

Every book demands a personal sacrifice that must be endured by others as well. In this case, I thank my wife, Pauletta, and our daughter, Jade, who put up with my new companion, the word processor. They offered perfect words of encouragement precisely when I needed them. Their support helped me to better understand the love frequently mentioned by the golfers, the love that turned them into champions.

Special thanks go to my current and former colleagues at *Golf World* and *Golf Digest,* who, over the last two years, have helped me develop a greater understanding of this wonderful game. At *Golf World:* Terry Galvin, Geoff Russell, Alan R. Tays, Bill Fields, John Hawkins, Tim Rosaforte, Bob Verdi, Lisa D. Mickey, John Strege, Jennifer Cole, Jordanna Hertz, Lisa Vannais, John Antonini, Mary Bishop, Gary Van Sickle, Betsy Van Sickle, Pete McDaniel, Pete Wofford, and Trudy Hodenfield. At *Golf Digest:* Nick Seitz, Jerry Tarde, Roger Schiffman, Peter Farricker, Chris Hodenfield, Peter McCleery, Michael Johnson, Jack Russell, Mike O'Malley, Cliff Schrock, Scott Smith, and Guy Yocom.

Also, my gratitude goes to the writers and editors who gave me my start in covering golf: Al Barkow, David Barrett, Larry Dennis, Rick Lipsey, and Gary Perkinson.

My friends Lorenzo Benet, Tom Cunneff, and Joshua Peck, as always, contributed their support and encouragement, as did my in-laws, Peter and Barbara Sutton-Smith.

Thanks, too, to the players, their families, and their agents for supplying personal photos. A second thanks to the golfers' representatives for their assistance in arranging the interviews for this book.

Finally, I want to thank my publisher, Lawrence Stone; my agent, Scott Waxman; and golfer Billy Casper, who kindly contributed such a moving foreword.

PREFACE

The tearful embrace between Tiger Woods and his father, Earl, at the end of the historic 1997 Masters Tournament symbolized the journey through golf—and through life—the two had begun decades earlier. Only they truly understood the sacrifices that had led to that moment and what it meant to achieve the dream they had pursued together for so long. For all his remarkable innate talent, Tiger could not have done it without Earl.

The same goes for many other champions in a game that breeds a natural bond between generations. By taking hours to play, with many breaks in between shots, golf provides ample time for conversation between father and child. A father and son—or daughter—might play catch together in the backyard, but it's not the same as a round of golf, which emphasizes scoring and performance, creates a sense of honor and heroism, and provides a ready-made opportunity to establish memories that endure a lifetime. The game is a rite of passage for the father sharing his expertise with the child he is training for the future—the same child who will dethrone him at the first opportunity.

Many of the lessons that the golfers inherited from their fathers did not originate at the golf course. Some didn't even play the game. They were preoccupied with the challenge of survival. Yet the examples of hard work and fair play, of self-respect and respect toward others that they consistently set went a long way toward inspiring the competitive spirit, resiliency, and passion that became an integral part of their children's success. It is no coincidence that these sons and daughters, among the finest in their profession, exhibit the values and virtues that make golf such a noble pursuit.

At first, some lessons are not easily absorbed. They take years to jell, often dismissed by cocky youths who think they know better. Too often it takes the birth of their own son or daughter before they truly comprehend what had been misinterpreted or ignored for so long.

The golfers who tell their stories here have reached that level of understanding. They deeply value the lessons they learned and appreciate the sacrifices made for their benefit.

Their fathers will never be forgotten.

Michael Arkush

FAIRWAYS AND DREAMS

AMY ALCOTT

Amy Alcott first appeared on the national stage as a brash teenager in the midseventies, daring to dethrone women almost twice her age. She succeeded. For nine straight years Alcott finished among the top ten on the money list. Along the way she has captured twenty-nine official events, including five majors—the 1980 U.S. Women's Open, the 1979 Peter Jackson Classic, and the prestigious Nabisco Dinah Shore three times. Today it's her turn, as one of the game's elders, to hope for some final bows before giving way to the new generation of upstarts. Such a challenge is familiar to Alcott, who overcame some troubles at home to excel in the sport she loved from the start.

These days you hear so much about what fabulous dads Tiger, Arnie, and Jack have had. They all seem like typical American success stories, full of unconditional love and perfect harmony, a real-life *Leave It to Beaver*. Well, I, too, had that, but my story had a different bent to it.

My tale is not a sitcom that can be neatly wrapped up in twenty-two minutes. People talk about how I turned professional at nineteen, won my third tournament, and all that other great propaganda for the press guide, but there is another part of the story about which few people know. Dad had a gambling problem. My mother told me this many years later after she learned of it and at a time when

I was a teenager and on the path to becoming a successful amateur golfer. My dad, Dr. Eugene Alcott, an orthodontist who owned three practices in southern California, had made a good living, but his gambling jeopardized all that.

My mother had a gift for tremendous compassion and empathy, but she was not a miracle worker. She tried to get him help, but nothing seemed to work. Ultimately, a divorce was the only solution. While this was taking a toll on our family, I wonder how I was able to perform in tournaments as well as I did. I think my answer today is clear, that my father, in spite of his problem, gave me a lot of love and

I was blessed to have a father who let me know there were no barriers.

made me believe I was as good as any boy or girl golfer whom I came up against.

I suppose I should be filled with anger at how it disrupted my family. I'm not. Sure, part of me will always carry some resentment, but I choose to focus on the positive effects he had on my life. Strangely enough, his gambling turned out to be a blessing for my career. That same gambler's mentality, the restlessness and drive I inherited from him, helped me overcome fear and timidity to win golf tournaments.

IN THE YEAR BEFORE HE DIED, AFTER WE HAD BEEN STRANGERS FOR SO LONG, WE BEGAN TO GET A LITTLE CLOSER, AND FOR THAT I AM SO GRATEFUL.

It's an obsession to work at something when it's dark out, when you're sixteen years old, and when you're by yourself without a normal existence. I thank my father for that kind of mindset. On the way to winning my first Dinah Shore, my caddie said to me, "You're going to lay up, aren't you? You've got 190 yards into the wind over the water." I said, "Nope, I'd rather win the tournament with style. We're going for it. If I fall on my face, I fall on my face."

That gamble paid off.

I choose to focus on the positive effects Dad had on my life.

Years later, long after my parents divorced, my father came out to watch me compete. We didn't say too much to each other, but he stayed for all four rounds. To this day I wonder why we didn't reach out to each other more. But one thing is for sure: His little girl brought him pure joy, which I think was why he showed up. In the year before he died, after we had been strangers for so long, we began to get a little closer, and for that I am so grateful. It was almost as if we both knew there wasn't much time left, even though he was only sixty.

My fondest memory of him is when I won the U.S. Open in Nashville. It was well over one hundred degrees for four days in a row and his health was failing. Yet he was there to cheer on his daughter.

Whenever he did come out to tour events, he kept a low profile, as he didn't want to distract me. But at the Open, after I made a two-foot par putt on the final hole, for some reason I looked 150 yards down the fairway and I saw him standing in the shade by a tree, holding his arms up high and shaking his head as if to say, "My little girl has won the U.S. Open." He died six months later.

It was only fitting that he was there for the biggest moment of my career. When I was eight years old, he bought me my first set of cut-down golf clubs with a little plaid bag, which I still have today. He was the one who entered me in tournaments for boys only. I would say, "Dad, I am not going to play in these tournaments. There's no girls' division." His response was, "Oh, yes, you will. You are going to go out and have fun and do the best you can do." I was blessed to have a father who let me know there were no barriers, that I could do whatever I wanted to do in the world of sports.

I loved golf from the beginning. I used to watch it on television after the Saturday morning cartoons. The *CBS Golf Classic, Shell's Wonderful World of Golf, The Big Three*—I watched all those shows. I learned how to play by hitting balls into a net my father built in our backyard. We had a sand trap and a putting green in the front yard. I hit so many balls out of there that he had to take me to the hardware store every week to buy new bags of sand. Although he himself didn't play, he saw that I was falling in love with golf. He did whatever he could to support it.

The biggest thing was unconditional

Dad did whatever he could to support my love for the game.

love. He and my mother let me know that they would love me just as much if I shot 90 as they would if I shot 60. That was quite different from the parents of many kids I grew up with. Other parents would say some unbelievably insensitive things to their kids, like, "Why did you three-putt on thirteen?" or "You should have known to hit a five-iron to that hole." My parents didn't do that. In fact, they were ready for me to quit any time I wanted to. "Don't you think you need to take a little break now?" Mom said to me after I had been voted Player of the Year in 1980. "Your life is just golf."

I'M NOT SURE I EVER THANKED MY FATHER AS MUCH AS I SHOULD HAVE.

I'm not sure I ever thanked my father as much as I should have. The week of the Open, I took him out to dinner and breakfast a few times. We had some good talks. I think he knew how much I appreciated the things he had done for me over the years, before the gambling changed everything. But I wish he were here right now so I could thank him more intimately, so I could tell him that he remains a constant presence in my life.

Human beings are incredibly fragile. What we think is our greatest challenge isn't. It's usually something far more subtle than that. We all make mistakes, but if you look deeply enough, we all have special qualities, too. That certainly applied to my father. "Your dad is a great man," a doctor once told me, "and you make him very proud."

A few years ago, after the golf course where I won the Open in Nashville was destroyed to make room for a housing development, I went back to the same tree where my father had been standing when I saw him hold his hands up high and cheer with joy. I flashed back instantly to that wonderful day and what it all meant to me, not only to win the biggest tournament in the world but to see my father's pride in the daughter he adored. I tore a twig off the tree and remembered his smile. Everything else was forgotten.

I loved golf from the beginning.

BETH  BAUER

Beth Bauer, the 1997 U.S. Girls' Junior Amateur Champion at age seventeen, awaits a reputation only the future will reveal. Will she be another Amy Alcott or Nancy Lopez, producing a body of work that fulfills the promise of youth? Or will she fall short like so many other prodigies, forever mystified by the failure she had never anticipated? One way or the other, Beth will have to find the answer without her father, John, who died of a rare disease in 1994, leaving behind a daughter who became more determined than ever to make the dream they shared together come true.

I was only three or four years old when my father first put a golf club in my hands. My first clubs were cut-down woods that I dragged along on the ground at the golf course. My mom and he would go practice, trailed by this little kid aimlessly running around all over the place. I had absolutely no idea what I was doing, other than trying to imitate my dad. When he died, he was the club professional at Summerfield Golf Club in Valrico, Florida, and my hero. I used to hang out with him all the time in the pro shop, watching him sell shoes, give rulings, etc. There wasn't anywhere else in the whole world I'd rather be.

As I got a little older, he showed me the fundamentals of the game—the grip, the stance, the setup, the posture—all the things

I'LL NEVER FORGET THE TIME I REALIZED MY DAD WASN'T PERFECT. IT WAS AS DEPRESSING AS FINDING OUT THAT THERE'S NO SANTA CLAUS.

you have to understand before you even try swinging a golf club. Dad wasn't too worried about my swing; he knew that would come much later. His theory was to let the club swing me at that age and then, as time went on, the reverse would happen. It might not seem like a big difference, but it is.

I suppose he was grooming me from the beginning to be a professional golfer, although he wasn't like some of those obsessed parents you hear about who don't let their kids have a life. I kept other interests, like going to the beach and playing the piano and trumpet. I performed at recitals. I wasn't, as they say, forced to skip my childhood. I participated in the same fun activities other kids my age did.

I'll never forget the time I realized my dad wasn't perfect. It was as depressing as finding out that there's no Santa Claus. He was playing in a club-pro tournament in Orlando. I was standing

I learned early that I couldn't win every time.

on the first tee waiting for him to hit the ball a million miles and show everyone how great he was. His drive went right down the middle and I felt like shouting, "That's my daddy!" Then, a few seconds later, the worst thing in the world happened. The guy he was playing with drove it past him. I was shocked and confused. Nobody ever told me this was possible. I got over it, eventually, although I think I learned a big lesson that day: You can't win all the time.

When I was younger, I acted as if I thought I could win all the time. I used to get really angry and show it out on the course. After my dad had seen enough of this, he said, "When people look at you, they shouldn't be able to tell whether you're having a good round or a bad round. Either way, compose yourself and keep walking with patience and pride." I've tried to keep that thought in my head every time I get upset and realize that I am a role model, even at this age.

Dad and I spent a lot of time discussing course management. "Beth, just because you're on the tee doesn't mean you need to pull out a driver," he would say. "Play the hole backward." Out of that piece of advice came one of my strengths today—accuracy. I average hitting about fourteen or fifteen greens in regulation

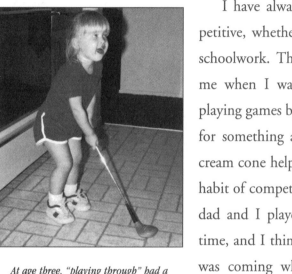

At age three, "playing through" had a different meaning.

per round. My short game is also pretty good, thanks to all the work we did on it. We chipped and putted until it was dark. Alignment was another important thing. He made sure I went through the same preshot routine every time, no matter what might distract me.

I have always been very competitive, whether in golf or in my schoolwork. That was instilled in me when I was very little. Even playing games by the putting green for something as minor as an ice cream cone helped get me into the habit of competing for a prize. My dad and I played matches all the time, and I think he knew the day was coming when I would beat him. When that time finally came, his ego wasn't damaged. He was proud of his daughter. We were a team.

Dad always knew the perfect thing to say to me. Because he played the game, he didn't get too down on me. I think he had some regrets that his competitive career didn't go any farther than it did. He played the minitour with minimal success before he took the club-pro job to support his family. I believe that's why he worked extra hard to help me. "Beth," he told me quite often, "I don't ever want you to think that you never had a chance." And the fact that I was a girl didn't change a thing. There wasn't a chauvinistic bone in his body.

The year I turned fourteen was a great year. So great, in fact, that I started to think I had a chance to be the National Junior Player of the Year. My dad, of course, was extremely excited. All the hard work he had put into my golf game was beginning to pay off in ways we had always dreamed about. First, there would be the U.S. Amateur, then college golf, and, if everything worked out according to plan, the LPGA Tour. He would be there cheering me on, just like he had always been.

Everything did not work out according to plan. My dad died. It happened so fast. Suddenly,

*I have always been
very competitive.*

he got this disease, Guillain-Barré syndrome, which affects the central nervous system. Nothing seemed to make him any better. Typically, as bad as he felt, he didn't want anything to disrupt my tournament schedule. He practically pleaded with me to play in the PGA Maxfli at PGA National in West Palm Beach. I had missed a couple of events already, and he was afraid that I might wreck my chances for Player of the Year if I also skipped the Maxfli.

I went on to win the Maxfli. I was so excited, I couldn't wait to get back home and share it with him. After rushing to the hospital, I entered his room and saw him hooked up to a respirator. Immediately, I realized that his condition had become worse than I had imagined. He couldn't talk. He just looked at me and slowly raised his forefinger to congratulate me for the victory. There really wasn't much I could say. He died three days later.

That was four years ago and it seems like

SOMEWHERE HE IS AWARE OF MY SUCCESS AND HE IS VERY PROUD.

yesterday. I've gone through the whole normal range of emotions, with denial and anger atop the list. *How could this happen?* I wondered. *Why would God take somebody so good from the world?* I used to hate it when, after playing well at a tournament, I would be approached by people who would say, "I wish your dad could see this." Well, as far as I was concerned, he *did* see it. Somewhere he is aware of my success and he is very proud.

Dad really cared about me.

WHEN I PLAY A ROUND, EITHER FOR FUN OR IN A TOURNAMENT, I THINK ABOUT ALL THE THINGS HE TOLD ME. I HEAR HIS VOICE IN MY HEAD.

Thank God for Mom. I don't think the two of us could have made it without each other. She's almost like my main coach these days, reinforcing a lot of the same things Dad used to tell me. Sometimes I've gotten upset with her because she never competed at golf and doesn't quite understand the player's mind-set. But then I realize how much she cares about me and how tough it has been for her since Dad died.

It's not easy for me to go to the driving range at Summerfield. A lot of memories come flooding back. I see the same spot where my dad used to wait with a bucket of balls for me every day after school. But I don't shy away from that spot either. Why should I? I want to be as close to it as possible. When I play a round, either for fun or in a tournament, I think about all the things he told me. I hear his voice in my head. Playing the sixteenth hole is especially emotional. That was his favorite, a dogleg par-four with trees on the left, water on the right. It's a great hole. We put a rock and a flower garden out there a few years ago. The rock says, "John Bauer, wind beneath Beth's wings."

Having a dad who was a golf professional made a big difference in my game.

MARK BROOKS

Mark Brooks is one of the hardest workers on the PGA Tour. Long after his round, long after many of his peers have left for the day, Brooks routinely camps out on the practice tee or putting green in search of any small revelation in his swing that might make a big difference. In 1996, Brooks won his first major, the PGA Championship, as well as two other tournaments and more than $1.4 million, a most deserving reward for a son, who, like his late father, Hal, a Southern Baptist minister, has relied on his strong sense of faith to endure one challenge after another.

More than anything else, my father taught me to never be afraid of failure. I can't emphasize enough how important that is in this humbling game, where you fail so much more often than you ever succeed. All you have to do is look at the numbers. If you're very good in this game, you might win about ten tournaments in your entire career, which means you'll probably lose about three hundred times. That's a lot of losing. But thanks to my dad, I don't worry about that. It's no fun to fail, but if you have a fear of it, it's almost impossible to succeed.

Believe it or not, there are a lot of quitters out here on the tour. They're okay when things are going well, but when things aren't going so well, they're not willing to do what's necessary to turn it all around. You either have that kind of character or you don't. I'm fortunate that I do. I'm fortunate that my dad instilled in me a strong work ethic. That's how he lived. He had a tremendous amount of energy, which he applied to almost everything he did.

When he started out as a minister, there were only about six hundred members in his Fort Worth church. Eventually, there were four thousand. He wasn't a fire-

Dad had a tremendous amount of energy. My grandfather, Paul Griffin, is on the left.

and-brimstone type of speaker; that wasn't his style. But he sure could be a powerful motivator, and that's because he had such a deep and honest conviction. You don't have to be loud when it comes straight from your heart. Yet he never made it so that

> HE WASN'T A FIRE-AND-BRIMSTONE TYPE OF SPEAKER; THAT WASN'T HIS STYLE. BUT HE SURE COULD BE A POWERFUL MOTIVATOR, AND THAT'S BECAUSE HE HAD SUCH A DEEP AND HONEST CONVICTION.

religion consumed our lives. We went to church every Sunday, of course, but we also had season tickets to Dallas Cowboys games.

My dad was quite an athlete in his youth. By his senior year of high school basketball, he had become one of the nation's top ten recruited guards. He got a full college scholarship and played for the legendary Henry Iba at Oklahoma State University. So, naturally, Dad was quite sympathetic to my love for sports and made all the necessary sacrifices. If the regular cash flow wouldn't cover, say, three months of my traveling around the country to play in amateur tournaments, he would take out loans. Even back then, spending the money for me to play cost several thousand dollars. I was improving as a player and getting invited to more of these tournaments every year, so the expense only kept going up. No matter. He paid it and didn't complain.

IF I DESERVED THE BELT, I GOT THE BELT.

He and I didn't play together more than a few times a year—he was too busy at the church—but when we did, he was never overly critical. I think that was very important. He knew how fragile people were and how constant criticism could keep a kid down, perhaps forever. Even though I grew up as a perfectionist, and I still am one, I have never thought less of myself if I didn't perform up to my expectations or standards.

Being around coaches as much as he was taught him a lot about discipline, which he passed on to me. If I deserved the belt, I got the belt. If I did something wrong to war-

Looks like a pretty good spread.

rant no golf for a few days, I had to live with it. That same toughness, though, is what made him deal so well with life's surprises. He knew things could get tough, and he knew how easy it is to get frustrated and angry. I grew up understanding that it was okay to express those kinds of emotions, that, in many ways, you need that release in order to motivate yourself.

Dad also had a creative side, which I inherited. He liked to do some sculpting. I like to design golf courses. And, like him, I apply the same level of seriousness to every task, no matter how menial it might seem. Whether I'm lining up a fifteen-foot putt to win a tournament or preparing a pasta meal for my family, I make sure to respect each detail in the process. I can't stand it if I don't put forth a full effort. The only thing I can do halfway is watch television.

Sadly, my father died too young. He was only fifty-three when cancer took him away. By then, I was grown up, out of the house, married, and a father myself. As Dad became sicker, I couldn't understand why this was happening to a man who had given so much to so many people. He had led such a clean life; he should have had twenty-five more years, at least. For the first time in my life, I began to question religion. I never did quite figure that one out. I suppose I learned that there really is no great answer. That's probably what Dad would have said.

Not a bad-looking guy in the whole bunch.

JIM C4LBERT

—◦/◦/◦—

Jim Colbert's second career in golf turned out to be much better than his first. A jour-
neyman for most of his youth, Colbert reinvented himself as a star on the Senior PGA
Tour when he was in his early fifties, outdueling many of the same legends in the game
who had beaten him decades earlier. In 1995 and 1996, Colbert was named Player of
the Year, winning the money title both seasons on the last round of the last tournament.
His new status brought him the acclaim he had always desired.

When I was a boy, my dad and I traveled around the country together. We stayed in the best hotels, ate at the best restaurants, and entertained people in the best manner possible. As an electronics salesman, although he wasn't rich, he understood the importance of having the nicer things in life. From then on, that's what I wanted.

On one trip to Ottawa, Canada, the two of us ate lunch at a big, fancy hotel. It cost ten dollars, which in those days was a lot of money for a nice meal. They had a dessert tray with three different kinds of pie, and I thought how really neat this was. Experiences like that created a lot of drive in me, because I knew that for me to enjoy that kind of life on a regular basis, I would have to make it for myself; I wasn't going to inherit it. Not that my dad made a bad living. He did fine. I just have always looked for more.

> HE TOLD ME WHEN I WAS A KID, "DON'T BE LOOKING AT THE COACH ALL THE TIME. . . . YOU CAN'T PLAY LIKE YOU'RE GOING TO MAKE A MISTAKE AND THUS MAKE THE COACH MAD AT YOU."

He understood that. Whereas my mom said, "Well, it's better to be a big fish in a small pond than a small fish in a big pond," my dad encouraged me to dream beyond any self-imposed limits. I told Mom, "I want to be a big fish in a big pond," and Dad immediately knew what I was talking about. He was the one who always made me train and not stay out too late before a big match. He knew the sacrifices that were necessary to achieve things in life, and he wasn't hesitant to make them.

I'm a pretty confident guy. Some say I'm cocky, and I suppose they're probably right. But I also know that such confidence is among those qualities that make a good athlete. My dad always knew that. He told me when I was a kid, "Don't be looking at the coach all the time. You know how to play. You can't play scared. You can't play like you're going to make a mistake and thus make the coach mad at you." That advice, which I have tried to follow my whole life, is not restricted to team sports. In golf you have to trust your instincts. There is no coach! There is no one you can lean on in the most adverse times to tell you what to do.

While I've never been the most physically gifted athlete, I've known how to use everything I have. My dad was the same way. He was a very long driver for his size—he was smaller than me. But he could really rip it, poking it past the big guys playing with him. He hit it high and with a nice hook. He made three double eagles. I have never made one. One of the things I learned from him is that so much of your performance comes from your spirit, your absolute unwillingness to give in to others who might have more natural talent. For my first dozen or so years on the regular tour, I was just an average ball striker, but I could play. I could compete. I still feel like that underdog against the big boys, which I have learned to use to my advantage.

One of my great regrets is that my father and I didn't play against each other during a span of years when we could have enjoyed some really memorable matches. About the time I turned fourteen, he came down with back trouble and couldn't play for three years. By the time he was able to come back, I was already seventeen and much better than him. It would have been fun during those three "lost" years to feel the excitement of trying to beat him. To his credit, even though he couldn't play, he walked the course with me. That must have been very tough for him emotionally, to be so close to something he couldn't do. I'm not sure

Although he wasn't a rich man,
James Colbert knew about the finer things in life.

many fathers would have done that.

So much of golf is about setting up challenges. One night a friend and I wanted to go out so badly, but I had been grounded by Mom for some reason I don't even remember. Dad was playing pool in the basement with a buddy when we went down there to plead for a second chance. No such luck. Then, without forethought, I blurted out, "Frank and I will play you one game of eight ball for our freedom." Dad was never one to turn down a challenge. "Rack 'em up," he said.

Frank was terrible and my dad was pretty good, so our chances weren't that great. Dad and

DAD WAS NEVER ONE TO TURN DOWN A CHALLENGE. "RACK 'EM UP," HE SAID.

his friend would normally have beaten us nine times out of ten. Luckily, I went berserk, making every shot. By the time the eight ball went in, we were already at the door. Having something like that on the line was a total blast. I can recall that rush of adrenaline better than whatever Frank and I did that night. Over the years I've gambled plenty on the golf course for much bigger stakes. To this day, I haven't lost that rush.

The biggest risk I ever took, without a doubt, was trying to make it on the tour in the first place. I was trying to support a wife and three kids at the time. When I told my dad about it, I could tell he wasn't especially thrilled with the idea. "There's no money in that," he said. He was right. Still, he didn't try to talk me out of it. "Count me in," he said. He became one of six sponsors who put in two thousand dollars apiece.

His word meant everything to him, which he constantly reinforced in me. The five-year deal I made with my sponsors wasn't the smartest thing I had ever done. As I started to play pretty well after a couple years on the tour, they became the ones who were making all the money. There were a few ways I probably could have gotten out of it, but Dad was adamantly opposed. "Jim, that's not ethical," he said. "They're all good guys and none of them expected to make any money. You ought to ride it out for the five years." I did and never regretted it. Sure, it cost me a good deal of money in the short run, but it taught me a heck of a lot about honor, which is far more important.

Loyalty was another big thing for him, even if it came with a price. When I was a senior in high school, I got into trouble with our country club in Kansas City. I was practicing between the twelfth and thirteenth fairways one day, like I always did, when this guy in a tractor ran over all my golf balls, cutting them to pieces. I was mad. I flicked my wedge right in front of his

LOYALTY WAS ANOTHER BIG THING FOR HIM, EVEN IF IT CAME WITH A PRICE.

eyes and swore at him. I thought he was going to kill me. By the time I reached the manager, the guy, who worked for the club, had already been there to give his side of what happened. Suddenly, the whole thing was my fault.

As a result, the two of us appeared before the club's board to settle the matter. I didn't stand a chance. They had decided from the start that they were going to back their employee against the smart-aleck kid. I was going to be suspended for a few months from the club. My dad just stayed silent and listened to the whole farce. Suddenly, he rose up. "Fellas, my son shouldn't have sworn at the guy," he told them, "but other than that, the manager's dead wrong and the board's wrong and you can't

Don't you just miss those outfits?

suspend my son because I quit." Just like that. "Why did you do that, Dad?" I asked. He answered, "Son, I'm not going to have that on your record or mine. As they were talking, I was trying to decide if I was one thousand dollars' mad (the price for dropping out), and I was."

I can't describe how much that meant to me. My dad backed his son, not authority, which made me realize how much he valued my word. A lot of other parents would have gone along with the club. I've tried to treat my kids with the same respect. There have been quite a few situations where I've stood up for them in cases where everybody else normally sides with the teacher.

Dad remained one of my biggest supporters his whole life. Even when he was ninety, he retained an irrepressible, no-nonsense outlook on life. When I found out I had prostate cancer [in 1997], he showed his heartfelt affection

WHEN I FOUND OUT I HAD PROSTATE CANCER [IN 1997], HE SHOWED HIS HEARTFELT AFFECTION WITHOUT PAMPERING ME.

without pampering me. It was like the old days. Don't whine about your plight. Deal with it, he told me.

"You haven't had any health problems your whole life. Just get it taken care of. They'll cut it out of there and it will be gone."

Dad and me on his ninetieth birthday, October 1997.

BEN CRENSHAW

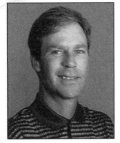

Golf fans will always treasure the image of a grieving Ben Crenshaw putting out at Augusta National's eighteenth green to win the 1995 Masters just days after losing the wise teacher who had meant so much to him. Harvey Penick first met Ben as a boy growing up in Austin, Texas, planting an admiration and love for the game that enabled his eager student to become a star. Crenshaw never forgot Penick and what he picked up from him, nor has he lost sight of the lessons he learned from another mentor, a man who showed him how to live off the course—his dad, Charlie.

I started knocking the ball around when I was six or seven, using a little five-iron that Harvey cut down for me. It was my first club. My dad, being a very good player—he was a scratch golfer for many years—was in a regular group at Austin Country Club, where I was able to witness some excellent play right from the beginning. One guy in the group had won the Texas State Amateur. I can't overemphasize how important that was. There is no substitute for mimicking what you see. Later on, when I played with them and hit a shot properly, I received such wonderful reinforcement. They were excited that I was learning the game, which motivated me even more.

My dad had taken a few lessons from Harvey, and therefore he had absorbed a lot of Harvey's wisdom, which he quickly passed on to me. Soon they became a sort of tag team, constantly driving home what the other said. I swear I don't remember them saying anything real specific about my swing. "Just wind up and hit it," Dad said. They were satisfied with my grip from the time I was seven. That approach allowed my mind to be uncluttered, with no thoughts about technical jargon.

Dad also possessed the wisdom to allow me plenty of independence on the golf course. He knew it was tough on me if I thought he was watching, especially when I was real young. So he stayed away during my early competitions. He showed a great deal of common sense about things like that. I think that also helped me develop more of an imagination on the course. I wasn't afraid to try something new. The best players in the game have always been creative.

Early on, from the time I started to learn the game, Dad felt it was very important for me to develop the social graces and manners to become a real gentleman. He taught me how to offer people a good, firm handshake and how to look them straight in the eye, giving them plenty of attention. It doesn't cost anything to be nice.

He had a keen understanding of how to make friends. Maybe he developed that skill

> HE WASN'T CHALLENGING MY INTEGRITY AS MUCH AS MAKING SURE I HAD ADHERED TO THE RULES. MAYBE I HAD MADE A MISTAKE.

from his long association with politics; he worked as a lawyer in the state attorney general's office. He showed me the value of friendship and not solely with your own peer group. I cultivated relationships with people of all ages, from eight to eighty. "Be as nice to everyone as you can possibly be," Dad told me.

Honor was also big with him. One day when I was ten, I shot a 74 at a municipal course not very far from our house. When I arrived home, he said, "You shot that? I want you to tell me about every single stroke in the round. I want to be doubly sure that is what you shot." He wasn't challenging my integrity as much as making sure I had adhered to the rules. Maybe I *had* made a mistake; we went over every stroke. He knew the course so well, I didn't have to write them down. As it turned out, I had not made a mistake, which I'm glad to report.

I had to earn things with my father. There was a Sears Roebuck catalogue with a catcher's mitt I wanted so badly that I pestered him about it for over a year. I thought if you used that

Dad was tough, yet very loving.

mitt, it would practically catch the ball by itself. Every time he came home, I showed him the catalogue. "I'll tell you what," he finally said. "If you can catch your brother's best fastball without being scared, we'll see about the mitt."

Well, that didn't happen immediately. I got pelted hundreds of times, falling down, scared as always. *There goes the mitt,* I thought. Gradually, though, I learned how to catch my brother's fastball. I learned not to be afraid, and Dad bought me the mitt.

Another time I wanted a rod and reel. Again, I had to earn it. That time I had to overcome my fear of stepping toward the pitcher when I was hitting. One day I got a nice hit off a very fast pitcher. Dad came over and said, "That rod and reel is going to be yours."

In a way my love for the history of the game came from him. He bought Charles Price's book *The World of Golf* when I was about fourteen or fifteen. He never told me to read it, but it was always around the house. From time to time I casually leafed through it. Then, when I was about fifteen, he talked to me about how the USGA Juniors would be at The Country Club in Brookline, Massachusetts, the following year and how that was such a wonderful and historic golf course.

Ironically, at about this same time, the passage I was reading in Price's book referred to The Country Club where Frances Ouimet had won the Open in

1913. Reading a story like that inspired me so much. My arrival at the course a year later marked my first visit to a formal eastern golf club. It was also the first time I saw bent-grass fairways. It made a huge impression. My love of history and architecture essentially started that week, although it was really the Charles Price book that first sparked my interest. I can't be sure, but I think Dad bought it and kept it around on purpose so I'd read it.

That's how Dad was in a lot of ways—subtle and extremely effective. Like the time during my junior year in high school, when I was sent to the police station because a friend and I were caught with beer in my car. My father had to come to the station to pick me up. I'll never forget the drive home as long as I live. He didn't say a word. The whole thing was so embarrassing to him. He taught Sunday school, and now his son was at the police station.

I sat in the backseat shaking in my boots.

Dad taught me a lot about being a gentleman.

Finally, when he closed the door behind us at the house and started going up the stairs to bed, he turned around and just stared at me for what seemed like the longest time. Then words came out which haunted me: "Son, that was like sticking a knife in my back." Needless to say, it was a long time before I drank beer in my car again.

As tough as he could be, Dad was very loving. He hugged people all the time. Mom was the same way. One day when I was about nine and I couldn't find anyone with whom to play golf, I went by myself to our municipal course. I played about eight holes when I suddenly saw my mother come over the hill. For a second I was worried that something might be wrong. "Benny," she said, "I knew you were going to be alone. I just wanted to come and spend time with you." That moment has always remained with me, symbolic of the kind of love and support both my parents showed me over and over.

JAY D6LSING

Jay Delsing wasn't the first professional athlete in his family. His father, Jim, played eight years in the big leagues, patrolling the outfield with the likes of Joe DiMaggio and Al Kaline in the late forties and early fifties, posting a record of achievement that would someday inspire his son to attain similar heights in his chosen profession. Through his first thirteen years on the PGA Tour, Delsing had earned more than $1.7 million. More significantly, he had acquired a sense of appreciation for his fortune and his journey, following in the path of a father who left his first love and never looked back.

One of the coolest things that ever happened with me and my dad occurred when I was about ten years old. The New York Yankees and our hometown team, the Saint Louis Cardinals, replayed their great World Series confrontation of 1949 in an Old Timers' game in Saint Louis. Dad had come up to the Yankees late in 1949 and hit a big home run that helped

them edge the Red Sox by one game in the pennant race.

That was the dad before I was born, not the dad I knew as a kid. When he came up to bat in the Old Timers' game, it was the first time I had ever seen him in a major-league uniform. I was filled with so much pride—and so much fear. I kept praying: *Please, God, don't let Dad strike out!* He didn't. He missed hitting a home run twice by a foot. I went nuts. That day I got to meet DiMaggio, Casey Stengel, Whitey Ford—all those guys. I see a few of them every year at a charity golf tournament. It's still one of my biggest thrills. "How's Jim?" they ask. They act like Dad's one of their pals, which he is.

> ONE YEAR FOR FATHER'S DAY, I SPENT WEEKS HUNTING FOR TWELVE OF THE SHINIEST GOLF BALLS I COULD FIND TO PUT IN A SPECIAL BOX FOR HIM.

I put my dad on a pedestal. From the time I was a little kid, I knew that I wanted to be just like him, a professional athlete, and baseball was my first love. I was pretty good but not quite good enough. So I started playing golf when I was twelve or thirteen. Dad and I would play after dinner until it got dark. One year for Father's Day, I spent weeks hunting for twelve of the shiniest golf balls I could find to put in a special box for him. He loved these secondhand balls and appreciated the effort I had made to find them.

The days Dad and I spent together on the

JIM DELSING
outfield DETROIT TIGERS

course were magical, giving us a chance to bond in ways that we couldn't in baseball. Maybe that's why I took up golf in the first place. It's not like we had deep conversations. Dad just wasn't that kind of guy. We never had that "man-to-man" talk. It just never seemed necessary.

In the beginning, like any kid, I couldn't wait for the day I would beat Dad and rush home to show the scorecard to Mom. He was probably an eighteen or twenty handicap. Soon I was beating him so badly that it almost made me feel lousy. It wasn't a contest anymore. But he didn't seem to mind at all. "Man, you're doing great," he told me. The fact that he took it so well and was happy for my success made me admire him even more.

What allowed him to be so content was the fact that he did something for twenty years that he absolutely loved, fulfilling his major dream in life. He grew up on a dairy farm in Wisconsin, left for good at the age of sixteen to play

My dad has been so content with life because he lived his dream for twenty years.

Class D baseball in Green Bay, and made it all the way to the bigs. It was quite a climb. It was no wonder he warranted such stature and respect in the community.

I hope I learn from his example. I look back at my thirteen years on the tour and think *I could have done this better* or *I could have done that better,* but I'm proud of what I've accomplished. If you look at other players from my first qualifying school who made it to the tour, not many have stayed out here for thirteen years. I tee up a golf ball for a living. I'm still living my dream.

Having a dad who played professional sports is a huge advantage. When things start to go well, he can relate to the pure feeling of achievement. When things start to go bad, he can empathize with the athlete's hopeless pursuit of perfection. You learn to realize you

DAD SEES LIFE AS A JOURNEY, NOT ONE MOMENT FROZEN IN TIME.

simply can't do it all the time. You play a sport for years and years, but you never conquer it and you never own it. That's especially true in golf.

As a ballplayer, he also recognized the futility of taking your problems home with you. His big saying was: "When the clubhouse door swings closed and you walk through it, that's the end of it." That was a real problem for me when I first came on the tour. I took so much home with me every day. I'm sure I inundated my wife with more than she ever needed to know.

Dad sees life as a journey, not one moment frozen in time. Nor is his life defined by the fact that he owns a 1949 Yankees ring, just as mine isn't defined by my membership on the PGA Tour. I have a wife and three daughters. They're my life.

My dad is in his seventies, and he's still doing his thing. He might not move around as well physically as he used to, but he still finds a lot of pleasure in every day. I hope I grow old with the same dignity.

A pair of family men joined by a loved one.

BRAD **7** FAXON

In June 1983, Brad Faxon, then twenty-one and fresh out of Furman, teed it up at historic Oakmont Country Club, near Pittsburgh, in the U.S. Open. This would be his last big tune-up before he embarked on the new adventure he had always dreamed about—competing on the PGA Tour. Faxon tied for fiftieth, an impressive performance for such an untested talent on such an unforgiving layout. Carrying his clubs for the final round was his father, also named Brad. Just seven years earlier, he had offered his teenage son a deal he would never regret. Together, the two strode down Oakmont's narrow fairways, savoring a moment they couldn't have been certain would ever arrive.

I'll never forget how wonderful it was to be with Dad on the same team at Oakmont. That hadn't always been the case. In fact, he used to make sure we were pitted against each other. I guess that was his way of pumping me up, of teaching me how to be as competitive as possible. If that was indeed his master plan, it worked masterfully. There was always something competitive between us, whether it was over one shot, one hole, or one round. He hated it the first time I beat him, coming up with all sorts of poor excuses. "Wait till it matters," he said. Yet on those rare occasions when we did team up together, such as the New England Father-Son tournament, we were very tough to beat.

Early on, golf was the best way for us to spend time together. When I was seven, he moved out of the house after he and Mom divorced. It was an ugly breakup. I heard each parent say nasty things about the other. On some occasions my father picked up my sister and me for breakfast, and he would not even enter the house.

Dad worked his way up to president of the gas company.

At twelve I finally spent more time with my father—a lot more time. I was living with my mom, but when she remarried and left town, I moved in with him. Dad was extremely busy with work, leaving me on my own quite a bit. Not that he really had to worry about a rebellious teenager on the loose. I was a geek back then. I didn't

I saw him maybe a few times a week, a few weekends a month. We stayed in a little cottage on the Cape, and I caddied for him in the morning and then played and practiced in the afternoon. Cape Cod was the best.

hang out at malls or party late into the night. I was so into golf I didn't want anything to get in the way. I didn't date until I was sixteen or seventeen, which is pretty late.

To his credit, he knew

WE STAYED IN A LITTLE COTTAGE ON THE CAPE, AND I CADDIED FOR HIM IN THE MORNING AND THEN PLAYED AND PRACTICED IN THE AFTERNOON. CAPE COD WAS THE BEST.

how serious I was about the game. That's when he offered me a deal. I was working as a busboy in a restaurant called the Wharf Tavern in Rhode Island three or four nights a week, and he came to me and said: "You know, your work is taking away from your golf. If you practice as hard as you can and go to the golf course after school, doing your best to get a scholarship, I won't make you work and I'll help you out financially the best I can." That was a huge gamble on his part because I could have just as easily decided to screw off. I didn't. I took it very seriously as a challenge to prove myself. It meant I could go after my dream.

> PERHAPS MY FATHER WAS MORE OF A ROLE MODEL THAN I EVER IMAGINED AT THE TIME.

Perhaps my father was more of a role model than I ever imagined at the time. After all, he had worked his way up at the gas company, step by step, year after year. In 1966 he started out by digging pipes, coming home dirty all the time. Today he's the president. It's not as if he and

I ever talked at length about his career aspirations. Like most kids, I was absorbed in my own world. But, as I look back, I'm sure that seeing my father move up in his line of work over the years must have shown me that dreams can

> EVERY TASK TO HIM WAS ALMOST SACRED. WHEN WE PAINTED THE WINDOWSILLS AT OUR HOUSE, HE MADE IT SEEM LIKE WE WERE PAINTING THE SISTINE CHAPEL.

Like most kids, I was absorbed in my own world.

WHILE HE NEVER HIT IT PURE, HE PARLAYED HIS TREMENDOUS WEDGE PLAY AND PUTTING ABILITY TO CONSISTENTLY SCRAMBLE FOR PARS. IT WAS A GREAT WAY TO INTIMIDATE HIS OPPONENTS.

come true if you work hard enough.

Every task to him was almost sacred. When we painted the windowsills at our house, he made it seem like we were painting the Sistine Chapel. He showed me how to tape the glass so you didn't get paint on it. "It looks like you're really trying," he said, which meant the world to me. I wasn't used to that kind of encouragement. It was a lot better than when he said "half-ass" to describe a job I didn't do nearly as well. To this day, I am like my father. If I can't put forth a complete effort, I don't feel it's worth attempting at all.

Dad and I have been through a lot together.

As an athlete you need to keep perspective, which is something I'm getting better at all the time. Maybe that is a sign that middle age is truly around the corner. When I was younger, I would let how I did on the course ruin me. With my dad's help, I've stopped evaluating my performance in the game as a barometer for my self-worth. Take the last two Ryder Cups as perfect examples. I was devastated beyond belief after the first one. I handled the second loss a lot better, coming away from Valderrama with the thought, *Look, I'm going to get mad, but I'm no longer going to allow it to consume me.*

Dad helped with the physical part of the game as much as the mental. Not that he was a superb teacher. He wasn't.

What I picked up came more through imitation. He was the club champion at Rhode Island Country Club in 1965 and 1966. While he never hit it pure, he parlayed his tremendous wedge play and putting ability to consistently scramble for pars. It was a great way to intimidate his opponents. I possess that same ability. I don't have to hit great shots to shoot a good score. A lot of guys don't feel comfortable hitting it all over the place. I do.

Dad was club champion at Rhode Island Country Club.

I took part in some great putting contests with my father and his buddies. After playing eighteen holes, they would down a few beers in the clubhouse, talking about life and women—probably some things that a fourteen-year-old didn't need to hear—and then we all went to the putting green. As the youngest, I was the one always put in his place. Each of them gave himself three-footers but I putted everything out. "Never pick those up," they said. I took it very seriously and it's a good thing. Nobody gives you three-footers on the tour.

WITH MY DAD'S HELP, I'VE STOPPED EVALUATING MY PERFORMANCE IN THE GAME AS A BAROMETER FOR MY SELF-WORTH.

Dad's my biggest fan these days. We've been through so much together, somehow managing to survive those early years when we didn't see that much of each other. I'm grateful that it's worked out this way and it gives me hope. My wife filed for divorce and I know exactly what my children are going to go through. I'll talk to them as much as I can about it, reassuring them that even though my parents also were divorced when I was a kid, my life turned out pretty well. My dad had a lot to do with it.

When we teamed together,
we were very tough to beat.

DAVID EHERTY

David Feherty is never boring. Whether poking fun at other players or himself, he is one of the most irreverent voices covering a game that sorely needs to take itself less seriously. Feherty blends a solid background in the sport—a Ryder Cup veteran, he played on both the European and PGA Tours—with an attitude he developed trying to survive in a country, Northern Ireland, which became a tense battleground between religions who hated each other. The terror he encountered in the streets of Belfast was not his only early introduction to life's hardships.

Before that day, I had never seen my father in tears. He had just been fired from his job with the freight company, where he was responsible for investigating claims involving damaged crates. Just like that, he was gone. No farewell dinner. No gold watch. Nothing. I was only ten, so I couldn't under-stand all the reasons behind it and its ramifications. But I was sure of one thing: We needed money. Lots of it.

Right away, on that first night, Mom mentioned that Dad was thinking about starting a business of his own. I went into action. The next morning, I stole some

DAD WAS AN ETERNAL OPTIMIST AND IT USUALLY PAID OFF.

rubber bands and staples from the school cupboard and brought them home. I thought he would be pleased with my efforts to help out the family. Not a chance. The next morning I was in front of my teacher, cap in one hand and staples in the other, with a carefully thought-out admission of guilt. The lesson was pretty clear.

Dad was an eternal optimist and it usually paid off. The business he started, for example, lasted longer than the company that got rid of him. I know he took a lot of satisfaction from that. My father, whose name was Billy, and my uncle later established a travel agency that is still running today. I developed the same positive outlook. On the golf course, no matter how bad things might become, I always believed they would turn around. If I could only figure out that one last piece of the jigsaw, everything would be terrific. I always knew that I would make the Ryder Cup someday. I don't know why. I just knew.

Looking back now, how I ever became a professional golfer seems ludicrous. I turned pro at seventeen off a handicap of five, straight out of Mr. Smith's geography class. I didn't even finish high school. What was I thinking? Still, although the whole idea didn't make much sense to my father, he said if that's what I wanted to do, well, damnit, that's what

I love you too, Dad.

I should do. He supported me the whole way. There's no question that I never would have summoned the courage to try to make a living in this impossible game in the first place if he hadn't made dreams appear so attainable and worthy. It's all his fault. Just kidding, Dad.

IT'S ALL HIS FAULT. JUST KIDDING, DAD.

Dad was really supportive.

He allowed me to form my own personality, free from the suffocating parental interference that often stifles a child's individual expression. I was very happy being by myself, consumed with all those crazy thoughts bouncing around in my head. That's probably why I took to golf. I enjoyed solitary experiences, such as when I kicked a soccer ball around. To his credit, Dad never said things like, "Why don't you go play with your friends?" or "You're a weird kid. What are you doing on your own?" He could see that I was absorbed in whatever I was doing and just let me get on with it.

Thank God he didn't try to mess with my swing. His was the absolute worst. He used this frightening Kawasaki motorcycle grip and swung like a club-footed lumberjack. A good shot from my dad traveled four feet off the ground, if that. He sort of bludgeoned it along the turf. If that wasn't enough, he doled out advice I had heard a million times before, things like, "Your head wasn't down." Gee, thanks, Dad. I hadn't thought of that one. Can you check my left elbow while you're at it?

At least he had the wisdom to buy me a set of clubs. I'm sure the fact that I kept turning his weekend group into a fivesome had something to do with it. He arranged for me to take lessons from Ernie Jones, the club pro at the Bangor Golf Club, about fifteen miles from Belfast. Dad let Ernie do most of the serious instruction, although he did instill in me the game's sense of honor. Whenever I cad-died for him, no matter how atrocious his lie might be in the rough, he never bumped it up. In every pro-am I play these days, some twenty-five-handicap bumps it

Where's the party? Oh, we're already there.

up or does something he shouldn't be doing. To me, that's not golf. That's cheating.

His sense of fairness and equality extended well beyond the golf course. Although we lived right in the middle of the civil war between the Protestants and the Catholics, both Dad and Mom insisted there was no point allowing some-thing that happened three hundred years ago to determine how you felt about someone who lived across the street. It was nonsense.

We had a Roman Catholic neighbor and my dad used to drink at his pub. Other people might not have risked that, but he didn't care what they thought or if that friend-ship might be used against him someday. He always said, "What a man believes in and what he earns are his own business." Perhaps that is why I get along so well with everybody, because my dad refused to allow any class distinctions to get in the way of establishing meaningful relationships. I'm as happy talking to the guy who shines shoes in the locker room as I am to the guy who owns the club.

> PERHAPS THAT IS WHY I GET ALONG SO WELL WITH EVERYBODY, BECAUSE MY DAD REFUSED TO ALLOW ANY CLASS DISTINCTIONS TO GET IN THE WAY OF ESTABLISHING MEANINGFUL RELATIONSHIPS.

Don't get me wrong, I'm not naive. That same pub where my dad went all the time was blown up when I was a teenager. A female police officer was killed. A couple of the bigger stores in town were also blown up. Things became so tense in Belfast you couldn't park your car and leave it unattended. Quite often, with all the troops patrolling the streets, it was difficult to get around. As a child, you felt those things were normal. Yet to grow up in that kind of environment, you had better have a sense of humor. If you didn't find yourself or the situation funny, you'd be constantly miserable and depressed.

I can recall the exact night I figured out it was okay to be a smart-ass. My dad had been drinking with a few of the guys at the club, then came rolling in for dinner about an hour and a half late. That didn't make my mother too happy. Although we didn't have much money, she went to great lengths to put together nice dinners so that we could all share a special evening together as a family. She was a wonderful cook.

Anyway, when he finally arrived, he asked, "Is my dinner still warm?" My mom didn't miss a beat. "It should be," she answered. "It's in the dog." I couldn't believe she said that. Her response made me understand that there is nothing wrong with talking to people like that. I had often thought of quick replies but never found the courage to say them. I've been talking like that ever since.

It was about the same time when I first learned the joy of performing in front of people. I sang in the church choir. My dad was in the congregation. He sang so loudly it was as if there were no one else there. It was dangerous to wear a toupee in front of him. It was a profoundly embarrassing experience at times, but over the years his singing grew on me because he was so passionate and uninhibited. He wanted to sing his way, and that's what he did. Why not? I began to realize: *Why not put it all out there? If people like it, great. If they don't, there's nothing you can do.* My dad put it all out there and so do I.

On your mark . . .

PETER JACOBSEN

Peter Jacobsen rarely plays the straight man. He wouldn't know how. Whether acting out one of his many impressions—nobody does a better Arnold Palmer or Craig Stadler—or hamming it up with the gallery, Jacobsen goes after the laugh, much like his late father. Erling Jacobsen, a practical-joke lover, taught Peter the pure joy of the game that would become his livelihood. Jacobsen will never rank among golf's upper echelon—he's won just six tournaments in twenty-one years on the tour—but he will always be a crowd favorite, applying the skills of an entertainer he picked up in his youth.

When I was growing up, Dad's phrase around our house all the time was "chip and putt, chip and putt." He was always going out to chip and putt. For a long time, I didn't realize what he was doing. When I caught on, I became hooked. I started out as a caddie for him. In those days his best friend when it came to playing golf was Bill Knight, Phil Knight's dad. Bill always complained: "I've got a crazy son. He's a genius but he sells shoes out of the trunk of his car. This kid's never going to amount to anything." Last time I looked, the crazy son was doing pretty well. (Ever hear of Nike?)

My dad wasn't one of those who forced the game on his sons. We all learned to enjoy it at our own speed. Who knows? If I had been pushed, I might not have learned to love it as much. Dad did a fair amount of teaching on the course, and a lot of it had nothing to do with executing shots. To him, how you behaved was far more important. That's why he had such a hard time with me. Many fans might not believe this, but I had the worst temper in the world when I was a kid. I slammed clubs and swore if a shot didn't go exactly the way I planned it. I was a big crybaby. I like to think it was because I wanted so badly to be the best.

Dad believed in not taking things too seriously.

MY DAD WASN'T ONE OF THOSE WHO FORCED THE GAME ON HIS SONS. WE ALL LEARNED TO ENJOY IT AT OUR OWN SPEED.

Whatever the reason, my dad didn't put up with it for long. Any time I threw a club, he yanked the bag right off my shoulder and told me to leave the course. That happened quite a bit. Once I did it on the third tee at Astoria Country Club in Astoria, Oregon, where we played a lot. I walked all the way back to the clubhouse through sand dunes that remind me of the ninth hole at Royal Troon in Scotland. For hours I sat by the car waiting for everyone else to finish their round. I was furious. Then it suddenly hit me. I was never going to get anywhere in this game with my horrible attitude. I was going to learn how to control my emotions if it killed me. Because of my father's stern methods, I did.

He taught me to maintain a consistent tempo, not only with my swing but also with my psyche. "A bogey on the first two holes is no big deal," he said, "because you can make five birdies on the back nine and shoot three under. You never know when you're going to turn a corner and hole a shot or chip in." I've used that approach after a poor start and it has worked. I haven't panicked. "You know, if you are ever in a tight spot," he said, "pretend you are hitting a driving-range six-iron or a driving-range wedge.

Don't do anything fancy. Just make your swing." That advice came in quite handy on those Sunday afternoons when the pressure began to build.

> STRANGELY ENOUGH, MY DAD DIDN'T LIKE TOURNAMENT GOLF. HE FELT THE GAME SHOULD BE PLAYED FOR ITS PURE ENJOYMENT, THE ALMOST ZEN-LIKE EXPERIENCE OF IT ALL.

Strangely enough, my dad didn't like tournament golf. He felt the game should be played for its pure enjoyment, the almost Zen-like experience of it all. My family always tried to persuade him to enter senior amateur tournaments, but he wouldn't give in. He couldn't figure out why I was so intent on competition. He and my mom both, as a matter of fact, were opposed to the idea of my turning pro. They talked about my becoming an actuary or an accountant because of my abilities in math. "Golf should be appreciated from within," Dad said. "Yeah, Dad, I'll do that . . . while kicking everyone's butt."

It's easy now to see that a great deal of his message was able to penetrate my thick skin. After every round, he asked me two simple questions:

"Did you learn anything? Did you have fun?"

"Yes, Dad, I did."

"Well, that's the most important thing."

I've won my share of tournaments over the years, and I've definitely won my share of money, but no matter how I've played, I've always tried to have a good time while also making sure everyone around me has an enjoyable experience. That's important whether you're winning the tournament or are on your way to shooting 80 and missing the cut. I don't ever want to lose sight of that.

Dad realized one of the ways to keep the family together was not to take everything so seriously. It became especially relevant in our family because, like every family, we experienced some pretty tense moments around the house, eventually leading to my parents' divorce when I was in my early twenties. I felt it was my job to make everyone happy and laugh at the dinner table so people wouldn't argue. Sometimes it worked.

The divorce became final when I was on tour. It became difficult to talk to either one of them—except on the golf course. You're out there all alone, far away from everything. You might as well say what's on your mind. We talked more about things in life—and life itself—than we ever did at home. That's one of the great things about this game. It gives people a convenient place to reveal thoughts and feelings deeper than those expressed elsewhere. As a parent I try to encourage my children to do the same. I show them a few things I know about the game, but I'm more interested in their lives. What's going on at school? How is the boyfriend? What do they want for their futures?

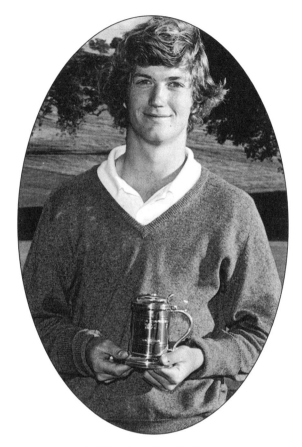

Golf has always been fun for me.

THE DIVORCE BECAME FINAL WHEN I WAS ON TOUR. IT BECAME DIFFICULT TO TALK TO EITHER ONE OF THEM—EXCEPT ON THE GOLF COURSE.

In general, my dad was not the most flexible person in the world. He was a conservative Republican with short hair, a coat and tie, and polished black shoes with matching socks.

He ran a strict household. But several things happened to him in his later years that changed him in very profound ways. One was the divorce. The other was when my brother Paul, who had a real problem with cocaine abuse, came out of the closet.

One time, in 1987, Paul didn't eat for three or four days and was running a fever. We were pretty scared. My wife, my dad, and I flew to Los Angeles on a midnight flight. I'll never forget the sight of my father sitting by Paul's bed, withstanding an incredible verbal barrage of profanities. The addiction was doing this, not Paul. The whole time, my father just sat patiently, listening to all of it, understanding exactly what was going on. Here was a seventy-year-old man who came from a generation where homosexuality was a no-no, where if you smoked a joint, you were considered from another planet, and yet he handled the situation with remarkable dignity. I learned so much that day about tolerance and understanding.

The way my dad fought death was just as impressive. Because of the cancer, much of his tongue was taken out, forcing him to learn how to eat and drink all over again. A special tube was inserted into his stomach to carry the liquid food he needed to survive. Sometimes the tube came out and I took him to the hospital to have it sewn back up. But he didn't roll up into a ball and quit. He didn't stop wanting to live. It was his will that kept him alive for nine years after the cancer was first diagnosed.

On his deathbed, he became quite philosophical, which was kind of neat. He spoke about life, his wants, his desires. You knew it was coming from the heart. One day we all gathered around him in the living room. The doctors brought him out of his morphine haze to tell him they weren't going to feed him any more out of the IV. It was only

> ON HIS DEATHBED, HE BECAME QUITE PHILOSOPHICAL, WHICH WAS KIND OF NEAT. HE SPOKE ABOUT LIFE, HIS WANTS, HIS DESIRES. YOU KNEW IT WAS COMING FROM THE HEART.

Dad's advice came in quite handy on Sunday afternoons.

feeding the cancer. As he came out of it, he smiled at us. Nobody knew what to say. We were all very uncomfortable.

So I finally piped in: "Dad, what's the most important thing in golf? The grip? The stance? What?" I expected some kind of monumental Hoganesque response, like something about the grip needing to be stronger on the left hand. He looked at me and simply said, "Sense of humor." That was it. We all laughed.

CAROL 10 MANN

Carol Mann took up golf at the age of nine, a lonely daughter in desperate search of her father's love. She became quite good in her late teens, launching a career that would eventually land her in the LPGA Hall of Fame. Mann won the 1965 U.S. Open and thirty-seven other tournaments during her two decades of prominence. With nothing left to prove to her peers and to herself, she left the tour in 1981. More than all the trophies and accolades she earned, Mann is most satisfied with the joys she shared closer to home, finally gaining the affection from her father, Louis, that she had long pursued.

Years ago, when I was about forty-five, I was asked to give a speech dealing with development, and I used myself as part of the story line. To get prepared, I went to my father to find out what he had thought of me when I was fifteen years old—as a golfer, as a human, and as a female. He couldn't come up with an answer. "I wasn't paying attention," he sadly told me. He certainly wasn't. For years he traveled all the time. He was in sales and marketing, peddling anything from Chevrolets to hamburger-patty machines. When he would finally come home, he would hang out with his cronies at the golf course, not with his children.

I started playing golf so that maybe he would spend more time with me. When it didn't work out that way, I figured it was my fault. I just wasn't good enough to deserve his attention. In a way, my dad's remoteness became a driving force in my golf. Perhaps I wouldn't have been nearly as determined to improve if he had been more forthcoming with his love. Who knows? He came to my practices from time to time but didn't stay too long. It had nothing to do with the fact that I was a girl. I have four brothers and he was aloof with them, too.

HE CAME TO MY PRACTICES FROM TIME TO TIME BUT DIDN'T STAY TOO LONG.

I now see that my father deserves more credit than I initially gave him for the golfer and the person I've turned out to be. Maybe he didn't offer me all of the time I craved for, but there were a few things he did that made a huge difference. Like making sure I took lessons. Not every parent does that. Although I was naturally left-handed, he told the pro to make me right-handed because he thought golf courses

My father deserves more credit than I gave him in the beginning.

were designed for right-handers, a myth people of his generation believed.

Dad generally stayed away from teaching me the fundamentals, although I do recall one tip he passed on, almost by accident, that enhanced my game for many years to come. By then we lived in

Chicago and belonged to Olympia Fields Country Club. It is one of the oldest and best golf courses in the country. One afternoon as I was practicing, he asked me what club I was hitting for my approaches into the green.

"Nine-iron," I told him.

"Well, let's see if you can make your eight-iron go only the same distance."

I looked at him and said, "How do you do that?"

We got along great during his last years.

It soon became clear: Grip down on the club and take a three-quarter swing. We tried the same exercise with a few more clubs. As a result of that twenty-minute session, I picked up an extraordinary array of new shots.

What he taught me apart from pure shot-making proved even more beneficial. One time the women's group at Olympia Fields decided on the morning before the start of a fifty-four-hole, stroke-play championship that they didn't want me to play because they were pretty sure I would beat them. They had the nerve to try this despite the fact that I had apparently been good enough at sixteen to represent them in team play for the so-called glory of the club.

I was stunned and humiliated. I ran from the first tee to the clubhouse in tears. When my dad found out about this outrage, he was livid. With his guidance, things were quickly arranged for me to make up the holes before everyone else started the next day's play together. That first evening after I got the shaft, Dad gave me the best pep talk ever: "Look, I want you to beat those ladies. (Come to think of it, he might not have used the word *ladies*.) You've been wanting a record player, right?" "You bet," I replied. "Well, I'll get you one if you beat them." I beat them and the record player was mine.

> WHEN I TURNED PRO
> A FEW YEARS LATER,
> THE FIRST THING HE
> SAID WAS, "GOOD,
> NOW SOMEBODY ELSE
> WILL PAY THE BILLS."

When I turned pro a few years later, the first thing he said was, "Good, now somebody else will pay the bills." That was his way of being funny, but it bothered me. It wasn't the kind of supportive reaction I was looking for. Mind you, he showed his support in other ways. "Where are you going to go to get ready for the tour?" he asked me. "I have no idea," I told him. In those days, there was no qualifying tournament as there is today. So he took immediate action, setting it up for me to work with Irv Schloss, a friend of his in Florida, who was then director of education for the PGA of America. His friend took me under his wing and prepared me for the tour.

I enjoyed a wonderful career and my father was certainly a big part of my success. In the span of a little more than two years, I won twenty-two tournaments. But I still felt empty inside. I called him up after another win in 1970 and said: "Rip"—that's what I called him, not Dad or Father. Rip was short for Rip Van Winkle. He was sleepy a lot when he was a kid. I said, "Rip, is this all there is?" By this point, although I didn't know it, Peggy Lee had come out with her song "Is That All There Is?" My dad sent it to me on the tour and I played it all the time. He could empathize with my sentiment that achievement, even in front of thousands of people, is not all there is in the world.

We got along great during his last years. I adored everything about him: his smile, his sense of humor, his intelligence. He lived until his mideighties. I miss him very much. One of the great joys of my life was getting to play a lot of golf with him after I left the tour. His cronies played along with us. Only this time I didn't mind. This time he gave me plenty of attention.

JACK NICKLAUS

Fans at first treated him as a trespasser who beat an American icon. They called him names and hoped he would go away. He didn't. Instead, Jack Nicklaus stuck around and became the greatest player of the century. From 1962 to 1986 he won seventy tournaments, including eighteen major championships, setting a standard that may very well last over the next century. Through it all, he has displayed an uncompromising commitment to his family, to a sense of values and priorities he inherited from Charlie Nicklaus, the Columbus, Ohio, pharmacist who gave him the opportunity he has never taken for granted.

My dad always felt passionate about sports. He was a very good athlete. In high school he played football, basketball, and baseball, set local records in golf, and was the city tennis champion. It didn't take too long before he introduced me to all the sports. We played tennis. We played pitch and catch. He taught me how to run. Every day he raced me to the movie theater, eventually goading me to try out for the track team, where I ended up running the 100 and the 220. He encouraged me to try everything.

Golf was no exception, although it came about quite by accident—my dad's accident. He hurt his ankle playing volleyball when I was five or six, although doctors didn't find a break for about two years. All the different medical procedures they attempted couldn't do anything to change the fact that if he didn't get active pretty soon, he might become permanently crippled. So in 1950 he took up golf again. He hadn't played for fifteen years, having given it up to concentrate on his drugstore business. I have often wondered how different my life might have turned out if he had never hurt his ankle.

I carried his bag and loved it. He was my best friend, my idol, the person I wanted to spend more time with than anybody else. Besides, by this point, I already knew a lot about the game from the stories he used to tell about his hero, Bobby Jones. As a kid, my dad had watched Jones win the 1926 U.S. Open at Scioto Country Club, the same club in Columbus where we belonged. He even looked like him. In 1931, when they played the Ryder Cup at Scioto, some people actually mistook my dad for Jones. One guy offered him a police escort.

I didn't learn much about how to play golf from my dad, except perhaps that he was the first to show me the interlocking grip. His biggest contribution to my future in the game was in simply creating the opportunity. He made it possible for me to take lessons from

HE WAS MY BEST FRIEND, MY IDOL, THE PERSON I WANTED TO SPEND MORE TIME WITH THAN ANYBODY ELSE.

WHENEVER HE HIT A GOOD DRIVE, HE WOULD SAY, "OH, I OUGHT TO BUY YOU A NEW CADILLAC CONVERTIBLE IF YOU GET IT PAST THAT ONE." WHEN I WAS THIRTEEN, HE STOPPED USING THAT LINE.

Jack Grout, who became the new pro at Scioto the same year my father again took up the game. I was ten when I started with Grout and I worked with him for nearly forty years.

My dad—who fluctuated between about a seven and a ten handicap—and I needled each other all the time on the course. It's a habit I still have today. Whenever he hit a good drive, he would say, "Oh, I ought to buy you a new Cadillac convertible if you get it past that one." When I was thirteen, he stopped using that line. By then I was driving it by him on a regular basis.

He made sure I understood that golf,

One of the best prescriptions in life is a round of golf.

or any sport for that matter, didn't come before family obligations. One summer evening in 1953, when I was thirteen, I shot 34 on the front nine at Scioto. Then I saw him head for the clubhouse. "Come on, Dad, we have to play the back nine. I have a chance to break 70." It didn't matter. "We promised your mom we'd be home for dinner. But if we hurry, we can get back to play another nine before dark."

I don't think I ate that fast in my whole life. We rushed back and I did break 70 for the first time, making a long eagle putt on the last hole for a 69 just as it was becoming too dark to play. But I learned a more important lesson that day: I learned about priorities. Throughout my career I've tried to maintain the proper balance in life, never allowing the game of golf to take precedence over my responsibilities as a husband and father.

I WILL ALWAYS CHERISH THOSE CONVERSATIONS. THEY BROUGHT US CLOSER TOGETHER.

My dad was into my sports as much as I was. When I returned home from a basketball or football game, he wanted to go over everything that had happened. He cared deeply about all my activities and I knew it. I will always cherish those conversations. They brought us closer together. A few decades later, when it was my turn to play the adult role, I tried to establish the same rapport with my kids. Because they knew I cared,

they sought my involvement in their lives. We, too, became closer.

My father never hesitated to offer his opinion. "You should have hit Butler going to the basket," he said after one basketball game. "You took that shot from the outside. You shouldn't have done that, should you?" I couldn't argue.

PEOPLE ASSUME I GREW UP WITH A SILVER SPOON BUT THAT'S NOT REALLY TRUE. YES, MY FATHER OWNED A FEW DRUGSTORES IN TOWN, BUT HE WAS NOT A WEALTHY MAN.

He was right. Some might see this as a bit harsh, but I knew exactly what he was trying to do. He was motivating me for the next game, believing there was room for some improvement. I feel the same way. That's why I never became too complacent on the golf course, no matter how well I might be playing. There is always something to work on. Early on, it was my temper, although he took care of that in a hurry. One day, when I was eleven, I knocked an eight-iron approach at Scioto's fifteenth hole into the bunker. I was so angry with myself that my club almost reached the bunker before my ball did. Dad calmly walked over and said, "Okay, let's go home."

"Go home?"

"If you're going to do that, we're not going to play golf. It will be the last club you ever throw or the last hole you ever play."

Guess which one it was. The same thing happened with my son, Jackie, at Spyglass in 1972. Flashing back

to twenty years earlier, I issued a similar warning to him. We also never faced that problem again.

To improve, I needed to be tested in competition against the best in my age group. That took money. People assume I grew up with a silver spoon but that's not really true. Yes, my father owned a few drugstores in town, but he was not a wealthy man. Most years, he made probably about thirty or forty thousand dollars, so I'm sure the financial burden of my entering all those junior tournaments began to pile up. I certainly don't remember us all going on long family vacations.

He knew early on how important golf would be in my life.

My early summers in Columbus were spent working in the drugstore. While my friends played baseball or basketball, I was stuck behind a counter. I hated it. My father needed the extra help. Besides, it was probably a good way to show me how the real world operated. But when I turned fourteen, he told me I didn't have to work there anymore. He understood that for me to be the best, I had to practice, something I couldn't do standing behind the counter of a drugstore.

WE SPOKE MAN TO MAN, AS EQUALS. BECAUSE OF THAT, I DEVELOPED A HEALTHY AMOUNT OF SELF-CONFIDENCE.

Using that same logic, he steered me away from a career in pharmacy. He felt there were other businesses, such as insurance, for example, which I studied at Ohio State, that could afford me a greater opportunity to display my golfing skills if I maintained my amateur status. I'll always appreciate the wisdom he showed at such an impressionable point in my life. He kept my best interests in mind at all times. He sensed, even before I could, how important golf would be in my life.

My dad always thought about my future. What was my next step? And how was I going to get there? Although he knew so much more than I did, he afforded me total respect. We spoke man to man, as equals. Because of that, I developed a healthy amount of self-confidence. I learned to trust my opinions and not be afraid to speak out when necessary.

He was a very generous man. When Barbara and I were about to get married in 1960, we didn't have much money. I wasn't a pro yet and was earning only five hundred dollars a month selling insurance. That's not exactly the way to make a mortgage. Enter Dad to save the day. He didn't like to pay rent for anything. Neither do I, for that matter. So, he said, "I think you should have a house, and you ought to buy it." Which we did. Our first house in Columbus cost twenty thousand dollars. As a wedding gift, my father paid the down payment of three thousand dollars. It was the last dime I ever took.

He died a young man. He was only fifty-six. His death woke me up. In the last few years of his life, I didn't really work that hard on my golf game. Sure, I won some tournaments, but I didn't spend nearly enough time fine-tuning the things that require constant attention. His death, in 1970, made me understand I couldn't continue that pattern of neglect if I expected to keep playing well. I

I THINK ABOUT HIM ALL THE TIME. I THINK ABOUT HIM WHEN I DO WELL, AND I THINK ABOUT HIM WHEN I DO POORLY.

went back to work, laying the foundation for what turned out to be the best decade of my career. I wish he had been alive to see it.

I think about him all the time. I think about him when I do well, and I think about him when I do poorly. He always

Actually, I didn't learn much about how to play golf from Dad, although he helped me get the finest instruction.

told me to admit when I don't play well and not to look for any excuses. I should take it like a man and move on. He was right, although it's never easy to explain a bad round to the press. If it were, then it would mean I didn't care enough. But I've done it. I've done it when it has absolutely killed me inside. I've done what my dad taught me.

DAVID  OGRIN

David Ogrin is a grinder who had always strived for one glimpse of greatness—the one week that would reward him for a lifetime of sacrifice. That week finally came in October 1996, when Ogrin won his first official PGA Tour event—the LaCantera Texas Open—after 404 losing starts over fourteen long seasons. His sense of commitment, which rarely wavered during the whole struggle, is nothing new in the Ogrin family. His father, Albin, a steelworker for thirty-seven years, belonged to the selfless generation that fought in World War II and worked hard at their jobs to create a better life for their children.

As a steelworker, Dad was a big union man, a Richard Daley/John Kennedy/ Harry Truman, old-style Democrat with an acute awareness of the haves and have-nots in society. Being the son of eastern European immigrants, he was definitely not a part of the privileged class. Nonetheless, my father never saw himself as being inferior to those with more money or better connections. He never thought he was one of the have-nots. If he felt any jealousy, he dealt with it in the best way possible, by beating the rich kids at their own game—golf. People respect a winner.

My dad spent a lot of time helping others because he considered himself fortunate. Every winter in north Chicago, not far from our home in Waukegan, Illinois, some folks would put up a net in a big auditorium so

MY DAD SPENT A LOT OF TIME HELPING OTHERS BECAUSE HE CONSIDERED HIMSELF FORTUNATE.

people could work there on their golf games. Dad volunteered his time to give lessons, and later in his life, he handed out golf balls to the kids. Some of that selflessness has rubbed off on me. It's not like I go out of my way to bolster the downtrodden, but I do give away clubs, gloves, shoes, and hats to junior golfers. That's better than doing nothing.

My dad joined U.S. Steel after he returned from the war. He never saw combat. As he liked to put it, "I was in Belgium, peeling potatoes. Got on a ship, went to the Canal, Truman threw the bomb, the Japs heard I was coming, and they surrendered." That was his brand of humor, a lot like mine—blunt and delivered with a straight face. He was the last child of four, the runt of his family, the clown.

I grew up in awe of him. He was my first hero. In 1957 he won the Chick Evans Amateur Championship, which was about the second or third most important amateur event in the state (incidentally, I won it exactly twenty years later). He hit big sweeping hooks that ran on the ground forever. I thought nobody hit it farther than Dad and, of course, every kid wants to be like his dad.

Once during a vacation in California, we stopped at Bermuda Dunes in the desert, one of the courses used for the Bob Hope tournament. He came back from the

My father was my first hero.

HE CAME BACK FROM THE ROUND ON CLOUD NINE BECAUSE HE HAD FOUND OUT THAT HE HIT AN EIGHT-IRON APPROACH ON THE SAME HOLE WHERE JACK NICKLAUS NEEDED A FIVE-IRON. THAT WAS MY DAD, HITTING LESS CLUB TO THE GREEN THAN NICKLAUS!

round on cloud nine because he had found out that he hit an eight-iron approach on the same hole where Jack Nicklaus needed a five-iron. That was my dad, hitting less club to the green than Nicklaus!

To him the game signified much more than individual achievement. It was almost sacred. He believed a day at the golf course was never wasted in any way, shape, or form. It wasn't possible. Maybe he felt that way because he worked so hard in the steel mills. Whatever the reason, I've tried to adopt the same attitude. I feel like I waste hours when I mow the lawn or repair something, but I can go to the golf course when it's raining and watch the guys play gin and not feel like I wasted one second. Go figure.

In taking the game very seriously, Dad gave me two rules to follow: One, never throw a club. Two, never withdraw from a tournament without his permission. He didn't want me to grow up a quitter. Do it once, he felt, you could do it again and again. "Do your best but make sure you finish it," he said. He was right, and I'm proud to say that in fifteen years on the PGA Tour I have never withdrawn from a tournament, and I never will.

My father was also serious about practicing. He never approved when I horsed around on the range. Over the long haul, he warned, I would develop bad habits. If I practiced without purpose, I would learn to play without purpose. These days I practice with a very definite sense of what I'm trying to achieve every single time I go to the range. As a result my practice is better and my game is better.

Dad was a tough disciplinarian at times. If Mom spanked me, it was one thing. If Dad spanked me, it meant a whole other level of sin. Yet at the same time, he never said, "You must do

HE NEVER APPROVED WHEN I HORSED AROUND ON THE RANGE. OVER THE LONG HAUL, HE WARNED, I WOULD DEVELOP BAD HABITS.

this," or "You must do that." I treat my kids the same way. It's very rare that my wife and I lay down the law and forbid anything. I believe the freedom we offer our kids—within certain boundaries, of course—will give them a better chance to develop their own creativity.

He was extremely poised. His basic philosophy of life, as he told me all the time, was, "Don't panic, pal." Of course, this was impossible advice to follow for a perfectionist, type-A, obsessive person like myself. I always had to

As important as golf was, family and golf were more important.

be the director of the universe. Panic was my favorite reaction. As I got older, his message started to sink in. When I won the Deposit Guaranty Classic in 1987, an unofficial tour event, I signed a poster and wrote in the caption underneath: "Dad, I didn't panic."

As important as golf was, it wasn't the most important thing in his life. His family and God ranked much higher. I was brought up Catholic. Without fail we went to church every Sunday before we went to the course. If we had a 7:30 tee time, we went to six o'clock mass. It's a good thing the priest was a golfer, too, because we were out the door at 6:45 and at the course in plenty of time. Once the Catholic Church started Saturday night masses, that solved the problem. Yet I'm glad we did it that way. It showed me the right priorities at a very young age. My dad's faith in old-fashioned Catholicism is what gave me the proper religious foundation that led eventually to my finding Jesus Christ.

Self-respect is another lesson he taught me. You wouldn't think of factory work as

> SELF-RESPECT IS ANOTHER LESSON HE TAUGHT ME. YOU WOULDN'T THINK OF FACTORY WORK AS GLAMOROUS, BUT HE MADE HAULING STEEL SOUND ROMANTIC.

glamorous, but he made hauling steel sound romantic. He loved what he was doing because he was making something that would last. When our family drove across the Golden Gate Bridge and saw the wire and big masses of cable, he said, "I could very well have had a piece of that." Of course, the bridge had been completed years before he started working, but we all knew what he meant. I try to approach my work the same way. I am proud of what I've done. Like my dad, I have built something of value, both with my career and, more importantly, with my family.

Family meant so much to him. He worked the graveyard shift for years and years just so he could spend time with his kids during summer afternoons. His typical routine was to get home

Dad's philosophy of life was "Don't panic, pal."

at 6:00 A.M., wake me up, and head over to Bonnie Brook Golf Course in Waukegan. We started at 6:30 and played eighteen holes in three hours. Then he hung out with us for a few hours, until about noon, and went to sleep. Every summer day was like that. They were perfect.

It taught me a wonderful lesson in how a parent should set up his life to help his children. Fortunately, I've found my own way to do it. Just two years ago my wife and I decided to take the kids—ages three, five, seven, and nine—on the road with us. We home school our kids. I know people might say they'll lose out because they won't be able to socialize in a bigger environment. We disagree. We think it's more important for them to be with their parents on a consistent basis, and traveling is what I need to do to make my living. I want them to have the same quality time that I enjoyed with my dad.

ARNOLD  PALMER

13

From the leading men who own private jets to the supporting cast who make a better living than they ever imagined, everyone who has profited from golf's remarkable growth in the last four decades owes it all to Arnold Palmer. It is Palmer, with his courage and charisma in the early sixties, who became the game's Elvis, molding it from an exclusive plaything for the upper class into a hobby for the masses. The King, approaching seventy, still is the most-beloved player in America, the son of Deacon Palmer, a greenskeeper who prepared him well for a most amazing life.

I did not grow up as one of the elite. Far from it. My father was the greenskeeper at Latrobe Country Club in western Pennsylvania. He was not an official member. There was a big difference, which he made sure I understood. It came through especially when, as a kid, I didn't enjoy the same privileges at the course others my age had. They used the pool; I didn't. They played a lot of golf with their dads; I didn't. I waited for the rare opportunity when I could join up with the caddies.

I wasn't too crazy about the situation when I was younger, but as I look back through the eyes of an adult, I have little doubt how much I benefited from that experience. It helped me grasp at a fairly young age that you have to earn things in life. You can't own what doesn't belong to you. The golf course is a wonderful privilege never to be taken for granted. I have played on thousands of courses all over the world and that is something I've never forgotten. My lower status at that club, I believe, has also helped me empathize with people less fortunate in life. Because of that, I have always felt very comfortable dealing with people at any level of society, which has greatly enriched my life.

At the same time I fit in very well with people on a higher economic or social scale.

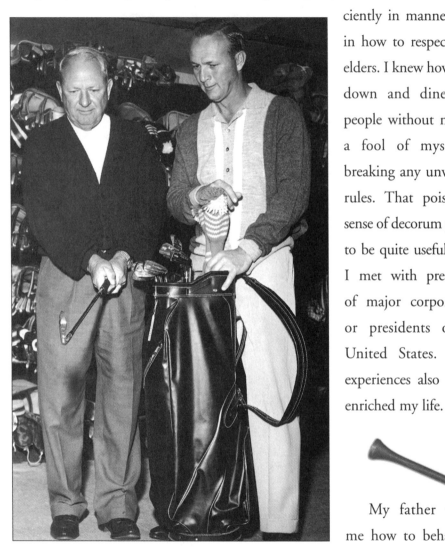

Actually, I was three years old when Dad first showed me the grip, which is pretty much what I have used to this day.

From the beginning, my dad schooled me proficiently in manners and in how to respect your elders. I knew how to sit down and dine with people without making a fool of myself or breaking any unwritten rules. That poise and sense of decorum proved to be quite useful when I met with presidents of major corporations or presidents of the United States. Those experiences also greatly enriched my life.

My father taught me how to behave on the golf course. Like most kids, I suppose, I

FROM THE BEGINNING, MY DAD SCHOOLED ME PROFICIENTLY IN MANNERS AND IN HOW TO RESPECT YOUR ELDERS.

threw clubs when the ball didn't go exactly where I aimed it. It was the club's fault, of course. My temper wasn't much of a problem until one day at a junior tournament in Pittsburgh. I was playing the mayor's son in the semifinals, when

Time to take a break, this time at the Fifth Annual Golf Gala at Latrobe Country Club in 1996.

I LEARNED FROM HIM HOW TO LOSE, WHICH IS PROBABLY MORE IMPORTANT THAN HOW TO WIN.

hole, where I made a ten-foot putt to win the match.

I jumped into the car and was stunned at what I heard—nothing. I couldn't

I missed about a two-foot putt on the seventeenth hole that would have put me one up in the match. I was so mad. Almost instinctively, I wheeled and threw the putter over a row of trees—and some people's heads. Fortunately, nobody was hurt. I then went to the eighteenth

figure out why. I had just won this incredibly important match against a tough competitor and nobody said a single word, not even congratulations. Finally, after what seemed like the longest wait, it came—the lecture. My dad was furious with me for throwing the club. He then

SO MUCH OF THE PERSON I AM ON THE GOLF COURSE COMES FROM MY FATHER. I HAVE ALWAYS BEEN KNOWN FOR MY GO-FOR-BROKE APPROACH, THE REFUSAL TO PLAY IT SAFE UNDER ALMOST ANY CIRCUMSTANCES. THAT'S HOW HE PLAYED.

said something that stuck with me for the rest of my youth: "If you ever do that again while you're in my house, you'll never play golf again." I knew he wasn't kidding. I never threw another club.

and integrity. Accept what happened, he said, give plenty of credit to the other guy without making any excuses, and get on with it. Then be resolved in your own mind that you'll do everything you can to make the outcome different next time.

I won a lot of tournaments, but I lost my share, too. Some, like the 1961 Masters and the 1966 U.S. Open, were much tougher than others. It took me a long time to get over them. But I always recalled what my dad had said and I made sure I was a good loser, even if I felt horrible.

I learned from him how to lose, which is probably more important than how to win. It's easy to do the proper thing when you win. Losing is an entirely different matter. He felt strongly that you had to lose graciously, with honor

If it hadn't been for my father, I wouldn't be where I am today.

I'm convinced that attitude made me a much better golfer —and a much better person.

So much of the person I am on the golf course comes from my father. I have always been known for my go-for-broke approach, the refusal

DEEP DOWN, I KNEW MY FATHER FELT A LOT OF CONFIDENCE IN MY ABILITIES. IT DIDN'T MATTER THAT HE NEVER SAID IT IN SO MANY WORDS.

to play it safe under almost any circumstances. That's how he played. He was a big believer in driving the ball at the flag all the time. As some in the press have speculated, it probably cost me a few tournaments. On the other hand, I believe I won a lot more playing that way. Similarly, when I've had to face challenges away from the game, I've gone at it in the same manner. When the doctors told me last year that I had prostate cancer, I opted for the most direct solution, surgery. I'm sure that's what my father would have suggested.

As for the technical aspects of my swing or the rest of my game, he didn't overdo it. When I was three, he showed me a grip that, believe it or not, is pretty much what I still use now, sixty-five years later. Other than checking it a few times, he left me alone. I was able to develop the flexibility to create my own style, which is very important. That's how you gain confidence.

My father couldn't do it all. He was too busy satisfying the members of the club. That's where

Dad talks to me and my wife, Winnie, before I tee off in the 1960 British Open at St. Andrews.

my mother came in. I owe a tremendous amount to her. She's the one who drove me to all the amateur tournaments. While my father was usually somewhat restrained in his praise for me— he might say "good going" or something mild like that—my mom never wavered in her support or encouragement. Every child needs that.

Deep down, I knew my father felt a lot of confidence in my abilities. It didn't matter that he never said it in so many words. I saw him show a lot of pride when he talked about me to others. I knew he didn't want me to get carried away with myself, which I believe has never happened despite all the success I've attained in both golf and in business. I can say, without the slightest doubt, that if it hadn't been for my father, I wouldn't be where I am today.

CALVIN **14** PEETE

Like Tiger Woods, Calvin Peete owes everything he has accomplished to the pioneers who endured years of prejudice to open a sheltered game to all races. Without the sacrifices of people like Charlie Sifford, Ted Rhodes, and Lee Elder, Peete, who won twelve tournaments from 1979 to 1986, would never have pursued a career in the sport that changed his life. Over the years Peete has shown his gratitude to his brave predecessors and to his proud father, Dennis, who taught him and his eighteen siblings how to get by in a white society.

Even with so many of us around, my father still found time for everyone. We talked at the dinner table and we talked after dinner. He told us all about his childhood and about the responsibilities he expected us to fulfill. Because he treated us equally, we never developed any rivalries. I follow the same pattern with my kids. I have six children from two marriages, and I'm proud to say that they all get along. They stay in touch and remain very protective of each other. As my father said, you may fall in love with other people, but you're already in love with your family.

We always stood up for each other against anyone, anytime, anywhere. When I was thirteen or fourteen, we were working in a cornfield in South Florida one day when the owner tried to mess around with our wages. He was prepared to give us only four cents a box after he had already told us, before we had started the job, it was going to be seven cents. All the workers were furious and looked to my father, who was the foreman that day, to make the situation right.

A lot of these people may have been winos and derelicts, but they could count. "Mr. Joe," my father said when he summoned the courage, "what you promised us is not what you gave us." Before he could finish his sentence,

We always stood up for one another.

instinctively, I blurted out, "Mr. Joe, you're going to have to whip both of us." Then my stepmother stood up to say that Mr. Joe would have to whip her, too. That remains one of the proudest moments of my life.

Mr. Joe headed to the truck to get his gun, but his partner called him off. Frankly, we were lucky to get out of there with our lives. The whole thing was very disturbing to me because I had just moved to the South

Mr. Joe angrily interrupted him: "You calling me a liar?" He then called my father a nigger and threatened to whip him. Suddenly, almost from Detroit, and I had never experienced this kind of blatant racism before. On the positive side, the incident showed me that my father was

HE ALWAYS TOLD ME, "CALVIN, YOU'VE GOT TO BE BETTER THAN THE WHITE BOY JUST TO GET ALONG."

a man who stood up for what he believed.

He always told me, "Calvin, you've got to be *better* than the white boy just to get along." When I was nine, he gave me an example. He asked, "Calvin, what is seven plus seven?"

"Daddy, that's fourteen."

He replied, "The figures are right, but the way you did it is not right." He said that if a white boy and I were asked that same question in a job interview with the president of the bank, the white boy would take a pencil and write the answer down but I would say it off the top of my head. "You've got to realize," he explained, "that the only thing the white system understands is figures, and they must be on paper."

Because I was black, I wouldn't be given a break. I would have to prove myself every day. I took that attitude to the golf course. I had to if I was going to stand any chance of succeeding. I didn't pick up the game until I was twenty-three years old, when a few friends took me to a course in Rochester, New York. I thought we were going to a clambake to meet some girls. When I found out what they had in mind, I didn't want to play. But I didn't feel like hanging around in the clubhouse all afternoon waiting for them. So I tried it.

I was instantly hooked. I even went to a range by myself later that same night. It didn't take too long before I decided that golf was what I wanted to do with my life. Seeing Lee Elder, a black man, on television competing against the great Jack Nicklaus in the 1968 American Golf Classic clinched it. If Elder could do it, so could I. I knew it would be a tough road. Most of the top players started at a much younger age than I did. My friends thought I was crazy and I didn't blame them. But I was determined.

MY FATHER DIDN'T PLAY THE GAME, BUT THERE'S ONE THING HE SAID ABOUT HUMAN NATURE THAT PROVED EXTREMELY USEFUL TO ME DURING COMPETITION. HE TOLD ME TO NEVER BET AGAINST ANOTHER MAN.

My father didn't play the game, but there's one thing he said about human nature that proved extremely useful to me during competition. He told me to never bet against another man. That advice helped to ensure that I wouldn't ever underestimate an opponent. Just because someone in my group might be going through a bad stretch of holes didn't mean I could lighten up for a second. I took every player seriously at all times.

I could never do what my father did for a living. But in my own way, I learned how to duplicate the type of effort he put into every moment on the job. So what if he didn't get paid that much? What has always mattered to him are his integrity and pride. He showed me that a man lives by the sweat of his brow, not someone else's brow. He always said, "Son, if you don't work, you're going to steal."

At the same time my father is not my hero. He is my father and that doesn't demean him in the least. I think, as a matter of fact, it tends to humanize him. He has made plenty of mistakes. But the important thing is that he has never tried to cover them up. His vulnerability and full acceptance of responsibility have in turn enabled me to admit

I started playing golf in my twenties and was instantly hooked.

my own failures, to not berate myself when I fell short of perfection on or off the course, as I invariably did.

He always seems to have the right answer. When I was making a million dollars on the tour, I started feeling guilty about my brothers and sisters who weren't doing so well working in the same fields where my father worked. "Don't worry about them," he urged me. "Help them when they are in need." His point was that I had responsibilities of my own, and I couldn't go through life trying to take care of everyone else's problems.

> HIS VULNERABILITY AND FULL ACCEPTANCE OF RESPONSIBILITY HAVE IN TURN ENABLED ME TO ADMIT MY OWN FAILURES, TO NOT BERATE MYSELF WHEN I FELL SHORT OF PERFECTION ON OR OFF THE COURSE, AS I INVARIABLY DID.

He taught me to be a leader, not a follower. I hung out with a bad crowd as a kid. We broke some windows, trashed some property—nothing major but certainly nothing to be proud of, either. When my father asked me why I did these things, all

> HE TAUGHT ME TO BE A LEADER, NOT A FOLLOWER.

My father has had great integrity.

I could say was, "I was with the other guys." That wasn't the response he was looking for. "It doesn't make any difference," he said. "You were with them. You were part of it. Don't be a follower." I wasn't a follower again. I've used the same line with my kids on more than one occasion.

Speaking of kids, I encountered some problems with my son. Like his father, he also hung out with the wrong crowd. I tried to help but, more than anything else, I made him understand that I couldn't be a crutch for him. He had to find his own way out of trouble, which, I'm proud to say, he managed to do. He became mature enough so he didn't need to run to me with every little problem, which is how things eventually progressed with my dad. If I had kept running to him, I would have learned nothing.

GARY  PLAYER

Nobody in the game's long and rich history has logged more miles than the South African known to his friends as "Laddie," known to the rest of the world as Gary Player. He is one of only four players ever—the others are Jack Nicklaus, Ben Hogan, and Gene Sarazen—to capture the modern career Grand Slam. All told, he has won nine majors. Even today in his sixties, Player, a fitness pioneer, flies around the globe with the purpose and vitality of men half his age, extending a remarkable journey for the miner's son who became a national folk hero.

My dad worked thousands of feet underground. He left very early in the morning and returned home at six o'clock at night. Sometimes he was there from midnight until seven the following night. I remember once seeing him come out of the mine sopping wet. You wouldn't believe all the water that poured out when he removed his boots. It was perspiration. They didn't have air conditioning in the mines like they do today. He had to crawl eight hundred yards through a hole about three feet in diameter, all the way clutching a mine lamp, with rocks right above him.

He took my wife and me down there once, along with Arnold Palmer and his wife and IMG's Mark McCormack and his wife. Let me tell you I would never want to go down there again. To realize he spent virtually his entire working life in the mines really makes me appreciate what he did for his family. He was fifteen when he started working there. He had no choice. When his father died, he had to leave school to support a family of six, and it was the only place in South Africa where they would take anyone his age to work.

WHENEVER HE PLAYED GOLF, HE ALWAYS APPRECIATED THE BEAUTY OF HIS SURROUNDINGS. HE POINTED TO THE TREES, THE LAKES, THE MOUNTAINS.

I think it's because he spent so much of his life in the black hole of the mines that he developed such a profound love for the outdoors, especially the golf course. Whenever he played golf, he always appreciated the beauty of his surroundings. He pointed to the trees, the lakes, the mountains. He may have loved the scenery more than the game itself. That naturally had a lasting effect on me. Today, when I play in a pro-am, I'm very aware of what's around me. I realize how lucky I am to work in this environment and not make my living in the black hole.

My father taught me to always keep trying, even when I knew I could not win the tournament.

I also appreciate the value of financial security. I didn't have it as a kid. When I came home from school, I had to take my shoes off and walk barefoot because those shoes needed to last for years. I cleaned them underneath to make sure water never got in. I took the laces out and washed them. Those are the kinds of things you do when you don't have money. But my father never complained and neither did I. If it was good enough for him, it was good enough for me.

Golf was his great joy. He never missed a weekend. For years I knew he played on the mine's golf course—all the mines had golf courses—but it never really occurred to me to join him. I was too busy with my own sporting activities, such as soccer, swimming, and track. One day when I was about fourteen, he invited me to the course. I went down and gave it a try. Thank goodness. I managed a par that very first day. It was unbelievable.

I still remember the day I told him I was going to be a golf champion. "A lot of people say that, but not many do it," he answered with a

> I STILL REMEMBER THE DAY I TOLD HIM I WAS GOING TO BE A GOLF CHAMPION. "A LOT OF PEOPLE SAY THAT, BUT NOT MANY DO IT," HE ANSWERED WITH A PARENT'S TYPICAL CAUTION. "BUT IF YOU DO WANT TO DO IT, MY ADVICE IS TO GET GOOD ELOCUTION AND GOOD MANNERS."

parent's skepticism. "But if you do want to do it, my advice is to get good elocution and good manners." It was the best advice I ever got. I took elocution lessons at preparatory school. It helped me learn how to properly address people and how to have a proper command of the English language, which I'm still trying to improve today.

It has been a big help over the years in terms of endorsements. If you need to project something, you had better know how to speak. My father spoke five languages, including three different Black dialects. He worked with black people in the mines, so I suppose he learned their languages out of respect. You have to be able to communicate with people before you can understand their culture, and there is no substitute for personal contact.

Black people adored my father. To him, people were never classified or separated by race or class. Apartheid or no apartheid, that's how he felt. When I saw the love black people had for him and he had for them, it became such a great example for me. Many years later I invited Lee Elder to South Africa and we participated in the first integrated golf tournament ever there. My father and Lee shared a great respect for each other. By what he showed me, my father paved the way to make that event possible.

Even though we didn't have much money, he hired a guy named John, a black, who pretty much became part of our family. He took care of all sorts of odd jobs around the house, including the cooking. We couldn't pay him too much. Nobody was paid much in those days. He was there mostly, I think, for my comfort. With my mother gone— she died of cancer when I was only eight—and my older brother off in the second World War, my father wanted to make certain I did not come home to an empty house. He had the awareness to realize how damaging that might have been to me. John called me Little Toughie because I used to climb the trees.

> LOVE WAS, WITHOUT QUESTION, THE BIGGEST GIFT MY FATHER EVER GAVE ME. HE HUGGED ME AND KISSED ME ALL THE TIME. I CAN'T OVEREMPHASIZE HOW MUCH THAT CONTRIBUTED TO MY SELF-ESTEEM, WHICH ALLOWED ME TO BELIEVE IN MYSELF AS A CHAMPION GOLFER.

Love was, without question, the biggest gift my father ever gave me. He hugged me and kissed me all the time. I can't overemphasize how much that contributed to my self-esteem, which allowed me to believe in myself as a champion golfer. He was so devoted that he watched me practice for as long as it took. If I stayed there all day, so did he. I remember once at the British Open, he wore his raincoat and got totally drenched. But he didn't leave.

From my father I learned that you have to keep trying, that even if you can't win the tournament, it is better to win three hundred dollars than two hundred dollars. As a two-handicap, he helped me with swing thoughts from time to time. He showed me how to stay down on the ball, and he was such a good putter. But his real contribution to my golf game was just the fact that he was there for me. We talked about that all the time, how that type of father-son bond couldn't really happen on a football or soccer field.

In those days few tournaments were televised. When I played in a major, my dad followed the action by phoning the South African Press Association. In fact, he was so interested that he phoned to find out about every hole. Any time I won a tournament, he cried. He was very sentimental. Later on, when I became more successful, I could afford to bring him along. I was able to get him out of the mine. He had been there for thirty-five years.

Dad epitomized sportsmanship and respect.

While not a particularly educated man, he was extremely wise. He used to say to me: "When people have success, enjoy *their* success because when *you* have success, you'd like them to enjoy yours. You look them straight in the eye and congratulate them, because when you win, you'd like that same guy to treat you that way." Boy, few things could be more true.

I think Jack, Arnold, and I were great in this regard. We were like wild men when we played. We wanted to beat each other so much it was almost unbearable. But when we lost, and it doesn't matter how tough a loss it might have been, we still looked the winner in the eye, gripped his hand firmly, and simply said, "Well done." Each of us knew we would try like anything to win the next time. I think that kind of respect and sportsmanship, more than anything else, is what this game is all about. My dad always knew it. I don't think the game ever would have meant the same to me if I hadn't known it, too.

Dad looks on as Jack Nicklaus and I review our scorecard after a practice round before the 1963 U.S. Open at Brookline, Massachusetts.

DANA  QUIGLEY

Despite numerous state, regional, and even national victories in the 1960s and 1970s, Dana Quigley did not succeed at the next level—the PGA Tour. Yet, the whole time, one person never lost faith in Quigley's character and talent—his father, Wallace. The faith was rewarded. His son joined the Senior PGA Tour in 1997. On August 10 he finally made it to the top, winning the Northville Long Island Classic. That same day, Wallace Quigley died.

I thought about him constantly that day. Over every putt my caddie, George, said, "We're going to win this one for Wally." And we did. When I finished, the first thing I said on TV was, "I love you, Dad," and then I went to the phone to call my mother at the hospital so she could tell Dad that I won. That's when my brother told me. It's impossible to prove, but I truly believe his spirit carried me to victory that day. When you tell people about it, they think you're crazy. But this was the victory we had talked about for years and years, and I think that his dying was the only way he could be there. I was a different man that day. There was such a calmness I felt the whole round.

All along he could have easily given up on me. Other people did. For goodness sake,

I did sometimes. I wasn't making it on the tour, so I resigned myself to what other golfers in my position eventually realize: I took a club-pro job. Not a bad life. You're still on a golf course every day, which sure beats a stuffy office. I met a lot of interesting and classy people, and I think I helped many of them play better golf. I still played some, as well, competing in tournaments here and there. But I couldn't help feel that I had let myself down and, worse yet, I had let my father down.

ALL ALONG HE COULD HAVE EASILY GIVEN UP ON ME. OTHER PEOPLE DID.

Dad always found time for me.

That wasn't the way Dad looked at it, however. He never for a second expressed the slightest disappointment at what I had been unable to accomplish on the tour. In each of our phone conversations from the road, I told him I wasn't good enough to be out there. I was probably looking for him to say, "Why don't you just come

HE WAS PROUD OF ME NO MATTER WHAT HAPPENED. IF THAT'S NOT A FATHER'S UNCONDITIONAL LOVE, I DON'T KNOW WHAT IS.

home?" He never did, even though I gave him a lot of chances to think that I wasn't the son he had always wanted. He was proud of me no matter what happened. If that's not a father's unconditional love, I don't know what is.

The thing that impressed me the most was how he dealt with the fact that I had a drinking problem. He could have come down much harder than he ever did. He never yelled or lost his temper. Instead, he asked, "Don't you think you drink a little too much to play good?" He gave hints every so often, but he never said, "You are doing this," or "You should be doing that." He always left it up to me to make the call. It was a smart strategy because, like all problem drinkers, I had to be the one to decide when to stop. Not anybody else.

ONCE HE RETIRED, I CONVINCED HIM TO WORK AT THE CLUB FOR ME. I REALLY THINK THAT I HELPED KEEP HIM ALIVE THE LAST TEN YEARS.

I finally did stop one night in West Palm Beach, even though I don't know why. Heck, I don't even know why I had started. Perhaps I felt such low self-esteem that drinking kind of put me out of my body and into another one. I know that when I told my father and mother, they both cried. It was the moment they had hoped would come for the longest

He was the most nonchauvinistic man I have ever met.

time. I haven't taken a drop in more than seven years.

Dad was a high-70s, low-80s shooter, but he didn't really play that much. He was too busy. He traveled a lot selling aerodynamic parts for airplanes. Yet somehow he found the time for me. He made sure I took lessons. I was no overnight hit, believe me. I shot 106 at Rhode Island Country Club when I tried out for my high school team. I wasn't able to beat him until I was a high school senior.

> MY KNOWING THAT HE WAS OKAY PROVIDED ME THE FREEDOM TO PURSUE MY DREAM FOR THE SECOND TIME, THIS TIME MUCH OLDER AND, HOPEFULLY, MUCH WISER.

The best years in our relationship took place after I left the tour. Once he retired, I convinced him to work at the club for me. I really think that I helped keep him alive the last ten years. He was sick a lot, but the job gave him a place to go, a reason to get up in the morning. My mother didn't have to pamper him. He loved coming to the club and the members loved him. Five former assistants appeared at his wake and said how important he had been in their upbringing. They all came from tough families. I found out my father instilled a lot of pride in them, just as he did in me. It felt so good all those years at the club to pay him back for the loyalty he had showed me. Sons don't often get that opportunity.

Even then, he still wasn't through helping me. It's no exaggeration to say that I wouldn't have tried for the Senior PGA Tour if it hadn't been for the positive reinforcement he gave me day after day. This time I was ready to come through. He encouraged me to keep practicing and to enter club-pro tournaments. Just because I hadn't made it on the regular tour didn't mean my professional golf career was over. He physically kicked me out of the shop to go play. He knew that when I turned fifty, I was going to get one more shot at it. For years he prepared me for that moment.

When that moment finally arrived, my father assured me he would be fine at the club

WHEN I THINK ABOUT HIM, HIS COMPLETE LACK OF SELFISHNESS IS WHAT STICKS OUT OVER AND OVER.

without me around. My knowing that he was okay provided me the freedom to pursue my dream for the second time, this time much older and, hopefully, much wiser. I called him from the locker room at each tournament and told him, "We're really on to something. I'm feeling good about it." I knew that by the way I was playing, I was making him proud, which only made me more confident. Without that inspiration, I never would have been in a position to be a winner in this second act of my life.

Now that he's gone, when I think about him, his complete lack of selfishness is what sticks out over and over. He lived his whole life for other people.

Sometimes I wish he had thought more of himself instead of everyone else, but I suppose that wasn't the kind of person he was. Helping others gave him an inner peace and contentment. He was the most nonchauvinistic man I have ever met.

By the manner in which he handled my mom, he taught me how to treat women. If my mother wanted him to drive two hours to get

Dad never expressed the slightest disappointment at what I had been unable to accomplish on the tour.

fried clams down the Cape, he went, even if it meant that he missed something he wanted to do. That's how devoted he was to her. I try to treat my wife, Angie, the same way my father treated my mother. I have a great wife and a great life. So much of it is because of my dad.

JUDY RANKIN

Nobody dominated golf in the midseventies as convincingly as the LPGA's Judy Rankin. Not Jack Nicklaus. Not Tom Watson. Not Johnny Miller. Rankin won six tournaments in 1976 and five more in 1977, while becoming the first woman professional golfer to earn more than one hundred thousand dollars in a single season. When chronic back problems forced her to leave the tour prematurely in 1983—she was only thirty-eight— Rankin exported her knowledge of the game to network television. Today she provides commentary on men's and women's tournaments for ABC and ESPN. Rankin credits much of her success to her father, Paul, whose persistence helped his daughter become a champion.

When I was six, my mother and I spent summer evenings in Saint Louis watching my father hit balls on the driving range. It was that time in America, the early fifties, when driving ranges installed lights so that families would go there at night. Those nights were some of the nicest memories of my childhood. They went by too fast. Like any kid, I wanted to hit balls and show my daddy I could do it, and he let me. At the time he was very impressed by Mo Connelly, the tennis star. Gradually, as I began to show some natural ability, he began to see the potential for me to become a good amateur golfer. All he was looking for was for me to have a better life. Turning pro, in those days at least, was not in his wildest dreams.

Right at this time, though, my mom was becoming very sick. She was diagnosed with a malignant brain tumor. You would think that her illness might make my father concentrate more on her and for-

When Mom got sick, Dad lost his heart for playing golf.

MY FATHER APPROACHED GOLF IN A VERY RIGID MANNER. HE IDOLIZED BEN HOGAN AND THE WAY HOGAN PLAYED, WHICH HAD A LOT TO DO WITH HOW HE TRIED TO TEACH ME.

his whole life after she got sick, and he was some-one who derived so much plea-sure from playing.

get about my golf. That wasn't the case. If anything, it made him more determined than ever to help me achieve my potential. He was very worried about me, about how I was coping with the whole situation. He also lost his heart for playing himself. He probably hit fifty balls

She died when I was eleven.

My father approached golf in a very rigid man-ner. He idolized Ben Hogan and the way Hogan played, which had a lot to do with how he tried to teach me. Hogan made him believe in the possi-bility of flawlessly playing the game: If you did things a certain way over and over, they would always come out right. In practice, for example, whenever I missed a green, he made me hit my approach shot again and again until I got it on. I used to hit my driver to this long par-three at the Triple A Golf Course. But when I didn't drive it, he sent me back to the tee. I hated doing that. I was so embarrassed. Years later we shared some good laughs, realizing it probably would have been better if I had spent more time learning how to get the ball up and down.

The strength of my game, not coincidentally, turned out to be accuracy. Fairways and greens, fairways and greens—I didn't miss too many of them. Because he was such a layman and never

It was because of my dad that I became a good player.

IT IS IMPOSSIBLE TO OVERSTATE THE SACRIFICES HE MADE FOR MY FUTURE.

had anything professionally to do with the game —he worked in the advertising business—a lot of people got the wrong impression of him. They thought he was too hard on me. Even I supposed he was once in a while, but there was never any doubt about how much he loved me and that he wanted only good things for me. It was because of him that I became a good player.

It is impossible to overstate the sacrifices he made for my future. For people of our income level—he took home a working person's salary—

it became quite costly to pay for five or six cross-country trips a year so a daughter could play in amateur golf tournaments. By itself, my mother's illness was debilitating financially. My father liked to say that before my mother became sick, the only debt he had in the world was the monthly payment he was making on his car.

Given all those circumstances, he somehow found a way. Naturally, I had to live up to my part of the bargain. I had to practice, which wasn't always so easy. There were many distractions as a teenager. I thank him for his perseverance because I don't know that I would have had the fortitude on my own to

Dad went out of his way to help me with golf but always left me room to breathe.

> I THANK HIM FOR HIS PERSEVERANCE BECAUSE I DON'T KNOW THAT I WOULD HAVE HAD THE FORTITUDE ON MY OWN TO STICK WITH IT.

stick with it. He always said that I didn't have to play golf, but if I did, I had to do the very best I could.

To his credit, he gave me room to breathe. You can't develop any independence when your father is hanging around you all the time. Every now and then, he showed up at a tournament, but for the most part he put me out there on my own to succeed. I've always appreciated that. Even at seventeen or eighteen, I was a responsible kid who didn't get into any trouble. He knew that, so he could assume that I would be safe.

He was never far away from the phone in case I needed him. We talked all the time. "What do you mean, you're scared of four-foot putts?" he said. "Get over it. Just aim at the center of the hole and pop it right in there." Remember, this was before the Bob Rotellas and Deborah Grahams of the world took over, when your father served as your sports psychologist. He was great at it. He often told me that he would do his best to never ask more of me than I could do. Although I sometimes questioned whether that was indeed true, it's clear to me now that he really got a lot out of me that I probably wouldn't have done on my own.

Last one in the pool . . .

For all his sternness and reliance on precision, my father was a dreamer. Back in the late-seventies he came up with an idea about how tungsten was so hard it could serve as a great insert for a golf club. He went to a tool shop and had this insert made out of a little piece of tungsten and put it in a driver. The end result was that the face of the club was so heavy, you couldn't get the ball into the air. So the experiment failed miserably. Yet today tungsten is used in some form or fashion in golf clubs. My father was no inventor, nor was he well educated, but he was very intelligent and extremely logical.

"WHAT DO YOU MEAN, YOU'RE SCARED OF FOUR-FOOT PUTTS?" HE SAID. "GET OVER IT. JUST AIM AT THE CENTER OF THE HOLE AND POP IT RIGHT IN THERE."

From the time I was a little girl on, he and I had these long talks that gave me a solid faith and a great deal of motivation. I think when you lose your mother so early in life, things become more serious, probably forever. It was always very important to him that I knew that golf wasn't the most critical thing in my life. He wanted me to have a somewhat normal existence outside of the game, which I did. I have worked hard to pass on the same kind of broad outlook on life to my son, and I feel like he's special. For that, too, I thank my father.

CHI CHI RODRIGUEZ

18

As a golfer, his credentials can't compare with his contemporaries. As an entertainer, Juan "Chi Chi" Rodriguez is unrivaled. Even today in his sixties, working on golf's version of Off Broadway—the Senior PGA Tour—his act remains just as hysterical. But Chi Chi is more than a comic. He is a savior, raising millions for troubled youngsters to start new lives at a Florida camp he helped to establish in the seventies. He is a lot like his father, Juan, a simple laborer from the village of Rio Piedras, Puerto Rico, who, day after day, set an example his son would never forget.

My father shared with everyone. We lived next to the main road of the neighborhood, and whenever he saw a kid go hungry, he always gave him his food. It very well might have been my father's only meal that day, but it didn't matter. He then went behind our house and ate food that came out of the ground, like raw tomatoes.

We didn't have a lot of money. We never had running water. One of the best exercises I had as a kid was when my dad said, "Let's go dig a new hole for the outhouse." We didn't have a table. We ate out of our hands. I drank black coffee in the morning and didn't see a meal until that night. There was no lunch in my house. Yet the funny thing is, when I was an adult, one time I told my dad I had a case of diarrhea. He said, "What's that?" He was never sick to his stomach. I really believe God took care of him because he gave his food to the kids. He may have been poor materially, but spiritually he was a millionaire.

C'mon, I saved a seat for you.

thinking. As busy and as exhausted as he must have been, he still never lost sight of the most important thing in his life, his family. That's one lesson which has stayed with me ever since.

He did everything he could to protect us. Once, two guys in the

He called every one of his sons "Don." There was Don Juan, Don Julio, Don Jesus. The sisters

> I REALLY BELIEVE GOD TOOK CARE OF HIM BECAUSE HE GAVE HIS FOOD TO THE KIDS. HE MAY HAVE BEEN POOR MATERIALLY, BUT SPIRITUALLY HE WAS A MILLIONAIRE.

were Miss Carmen, Miss Maria, Miss Juanita. Every night, when he came home, he took about fifteen minutes with each one of us to talk about what had happened that day, what we were feeling, what we were

neighborhood who had just gotten out of prison made passes at my two young sisters, who were only fourteen and fifteen. My brother, Jesus, was a very fast runner so he went to get our dad, who wasted no time in taking care of the situation. With a rage you wouldn't believe, he found these guys, knocked them down to the ground, and took out a machete. He drew blood on one guy's neck and said, "If you ever come around here, I'll cut your head off." Needless to say, those

HE DID EVERYTHING HE COULD TO PROTECT US.

guys never bothered my sisters again.

My dad was very tough at home, too. Rules were rules and if you didn't obey them, you paid a pretty high price. When he said that lights were going out at seven o'clock, he meant seven o'clock. I'll never forget when my older brother, who later became a lawyer, showed up at 7:05, my dad said, "You don't sleep in the house tonight. You were not here at seven o'clock." He made my brother sleep under the house. My brother was never late again. Neither was I.

Although my father had very little education, he was the smartest man I ever met. He knew things that you simply don't pick up by sitting in a class-

ALTHOUGH MY FATHER HAD VERY LITTLE EDUCATION, HE WAS THE SMARTEST MAN I EVER MET. HE KNEW THINGS THAT YOU SIMPLY DON'T PICK UP BY SITTING IN A CLASSROOM OR READING A TEXTBOOK.

Olé!

room or reading a textbook. He understood the value of dignity and self-respect and how to pass that on to each one of his children. In his mind pride was something that could never be compromised. One time he went to work for some guy in the field. With a big storm brewing in the distance, the guy told him to gather together the cattle to keep them safe from the rain. My dad left the house at five in the morning and didn't come back until seven at night.

"How many did you find, Juan?" he asked my father.

"All of them except one. I'll go find her tomorrow morning."

"Go find her right now."

My father immediately jumped off his horse with a look in his eyes I had never seen before.

"Take the bristles, stick them up your a— and get her yourself. I'm through."

Just like that, he quit. I was eight years old, too young to really understand why, but it must

I have so much to be thankful for.

have made an impression because years later I asked him about it. He told me, "I'm a good man, son. I knew I could find another job. But I didn't want anyone to intimidate you ever. No man, whoever he is, should ever intimidate you." It was a beautiful lesson, one which I've always remembered. I have a tremendous amount of respect for Arnold Palmer and Jack Nicklaus. They were the best golfers in my generation. But I have never allowed them, or anyone else for that matter, to intimidate me on or off the course. That's a big reason for whatever success I've attained.

He always made certain that I stood up for myself. I was about twelve when I got into a fight with this kid who beat the hell out of me. I came home bleeding and my eyes were all puffy. I felt like a big loser.

"What happened?" my dad wanted to know.

"I fought this kid and lost. I had a good fight but I lost."

"Did you back off, son?"

"No."

"Then you didn't lose. You were not prepared to fight him. I'm going to teach you how to fight."

That's exactly what he did. For six months he trained me how to box. My dad packed the biggest punch I ever saw, which is how he knocked down those guys who were trying to fool around with my sisters. He gained much of his strength from all the years of hard labor. I think he could have been a middleweight champion if he had decided to become a boxer. I never developed the same kind of punching ability, but, thanks to him, I learned how to defend myself.

My father was too poor to play golf, too busy trying to raise us. He talked to us all the time about getting an education. It wasn't easy for me when I told him I was going to drop out of high school to defend the United States in Korea like many of my friends were doing.

"If you don't go to school, you'll always be a bum," he told me.

"Dad, you had only a fourth-grade education and you're not a bum. You're my idol."

He smiled and shook my hand. "Good decision or not, you've made it and you're going to have to live with it. You are now a man."

> MY FATHER WAS TOO POOR TO PLAY GOLF, TOO BUSY TRYING TO RAISE US. HE TALKED TO US ALL THE TIME ABOUT GETTING AN EDUCATION.

I didn't recognize it at the time but my dad was teaching me responsibility. The reality that nobody is going to hold your hand in this world is something I picked up very early in my life. Ultimately, I didn't go to Korea. I was lying about my age—I was only sixteen—and the government found out. Thank goodness. It probably saved my life. By the time I was old enough, the war was over. Many of my friends never came back.

In whatever job he did, he never complained. He just did it. For many years he washed dishes for a living, hardly the world's most glamorous or well-paying occupation. He worked six, seven days a week, and probably never took home more than eighteen dollars a day. I might earn more at a one-day clinic than he made in a year! Yet he always took the time to make sure everything he did was right.

My father died the week after I won my first tournament, the Denver Open. He was too sick to attend. But he is still with me. I dream of him all the time. I dream that we're together, enjoying our money, and I'm providing

I DREAM OF HIM ALL THE TIME. I DREAM THAT WE'RE TOGETHER, ENJOYING OUR MONEY, AND I'M PROVIDING HIM WITH EVERYTHING HE NEEDS.

him with everything he needs. He is the reason I live this incredible life, doing something I love and seeing the world. It is because of him that I never forget my roots. I also can't stand to see any child go hungry or live in fear.

That's why I started the Chi Chi Rodriguez Youth Foundation more than twenty years ago. We do whatever we can to give a new beginning to these kids, many of whom have been sexually abused. They play golf and learn important business and academic skills, so they will have a chance to make it in society when they leave us. We teach them manners and build up their self-esteem. We give them unconditional love.

CHARLIE  RYMER

19

By the yardsticks used to measure success in his profession, Charlie Rymer rates far below the majority of his peers on the PGA Tour. He hasn't won [through 1997] and he hasn't made much money. He has trouble just holding on to his playing card. Such mediocrity might do permanent damage to any proud professional. Not Rymer. If he never tees it up in another golf tournament, he is already a winner, overcoming the departure of a father who left home when Rymer was just a boy. A new role model soon took his place, giving him the stable environment necessary to make it in the outside world.

My stepdad, Jim, is the greatest man in the world. I don't know how I would have grown up if he hadn't come along. I don't even like to think about it. He came in and took over with no complaints, doing whatever was asked of him to make sure I led as normal a life as possible. That fact alone probably has done more to teach me gratitude than anything else. I don't take anything for granted.

We played golf every weekend when I was growing up in South Carolina, and there was always something on the line. It was usually my stepdad and me against his buddies, who were all good players, anywhere from five to twelve handicaps. If you didn't play well, you lost a pretty good chunk of change, maybe a few hundred dollars. He covered me—most teenagers don't make that kind of money—but if we won, he gave me a small percentage of the pot. The first time I ever broke 70, I was thirteen years old. I shot a 69. All I remember about that day is that we ran into some people who outhustled us and we lost about four hundred dollars. So much for the thrill of breaking 70.

Some folks might think gambling, especially for a kid, is a sickness and even corrupts such an honorable sport. They might have a point. But it sure toughened me up in ways that don't happen when you play merely for the love of the game. Nothing like the fear of losing your own money—or, better yet, your dad's

Good move, Mom, marrying Jim.

money—to make you concentrate on the next shot. That's exactly what you need on the tour when you're facing the best players in the world. You can't doze off for a second. The other guy won't, you can be sure of that.

Off the course I wasn't nearly as organized. Around the house my two chores were mowing the grass and taking out the garbage. Well, I could never remember to do the latter. All it took was two minutes, and I still would forget about it week after week. Once I was practicing with my high school team when the pro said, "You better get your butt home before your dad gets there. You didn't take out the garbage." I left the course in the middle of practice, rushed home, and arrived just in time. It was an embarrassing experience, but it sure beat the alternative, if you know what I mean.

Another time I wasn't so lucky. I forgot to take it out and, boy, did it *smell*. The trash was filled with the guts and heads of some fish my stepdad had cleaned the day before. Because the smell was so horrid, he loaded the garbage into his car to take to the dumpster. That might not have been the brightest idea he ever had. On the way he hit a big bump, and all the stuff poured out all over the car. I heard about this for a long, long time, although I never forgot to take out the garbage after that.

HE WAS ALSO TOUGH ON ME WHEN IT CAME TO MY GOLF GAME, AND IT PROBABLY SAVED MY CAREER.

He was also tough on me when it came to my golf game, and it probably saved my career. After I finished a mediocre senior season at Georgia Tech, I was so burned out with the game that I wasn't even going to try to turn professional. I figured I would find something a lot less torturous to do with my life and maybe play some amateur golf. When my stepdad found out about my plan, he went ballistic. "You have to go out there and try your dream," he told me. I listened to him and have never looked back. I figured out later why he was so intent on making sure I didn't quit. He was a very good catcher at the University of Tennessee, but, for some reason, he never tried to make it to the big leagues. He didn't want me to repeat the same mistake.

As forceful and articulate as he was, he also knew how to listen. He took the time to pay close attention to whatever I had to say, no matter how busy he might have been. I try to do the same thing with my family and with my fellow professionals. I know how much it

AS FORCEFUL AND ARTICULATE AS HE WAS, HE ALSO KNEW HOW TO LISTEN.

THEN HE HANDED ME A CHECK FOR ONE THOUSAND DOLLARS, WHICH BLEW ME AWAY. IF HE BELIEVED IN ME THAT MUCH, THEN THERE WAS NO WAY I COULD LET HIM DOWN.

means when they listen to me. Sure, we're extremely competitive on the course. But in the locker rooms and on the driving ranges, we're all in this struggle together. One day one person is down. The next day it may be you. If we don't listen carefully and pump each other up, who will?

It's so easy to get cranky on the road. I've seen many guys do it. I've done it and I'm not proud of it. But I know enough that when it happens, it's time to go home and remember what my stepdad instilled in me, that I am fortunate to be living my dream, competing for the outrageous amount of money out there, driving the courtesy cars, eating the free meals, doing everything else that's associated with this life. It isn't real. We *play* a game for a living! When I come to a tournament, I joke with the fans to let them know how happy I am. It's no act.

My stepdad has come through with more than just words. He has come through with

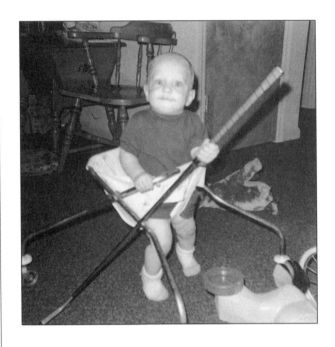

Gimme the two-iron instead.

cash. Once after I missed the cut at a Nike tournament in Alabama, I was basically broke. I realized that I had to go home and find some way to scrape together enough money to enter the next tournament. Or maybe it was time to look for a real job. I was down, way down. I had missed five cuts in a row—five Nike cuts, no less.

As I was contemplating all of this in the parking lot, ready to embark on my uncertain future, my stepdad walked over to tell me, "You've got to hang in there. You're so close." I appreciated what he was saying but, frankly, I

> NO WAY WILL HE EVER REPLACE MY STEPDAD AS THE PRIME MALE INFLUENCE OF MY LIFE, BUT AT LEAST I SALVAGED SOMETHING OUT OF THE WHOLE MESS.

needed more than a pep talk. Then he handed me a check for one thousand dollars, which blew me away. If he believed in me that much, then there was no way I could let him down. Wouldn't you know it? The next week, I won the tournament.

I'm so fortunate to be living my dream.

I'm lucky in another respect. As I got older, I was able to develop a relationship with my natural father who left home when I was only three. No way will he ever replace my stepdad as the prime male influence of my life, but at least I salvaged something out of the whole mess. Even more satisfying is that he has become clean, freeing himself from the depen-

dency on alcohol and drugs that kept us apart for so many years. He is a decent human being who just had a disease. He's even helping others with similar problems, as well. I'm very proud of him. He's been sober for eight years. More than anything else, his recovery has helped me see that people can be redeemed. Sometimes it takes a lot of hard work. Sometimes it takes years of unconditional love. Sometimes it takes both. For me, I'm just fortunate that my step-dad came along when he did to serve as my guide through life. I pray I can be as inspirational to my children.

Yeah, all the catches are ours.

JAN STEPHENSON

At a critical time in the midseventies, when women's golf sorely needed a facelift to compete with the more popular male professionals, along came a blonde Australian with loads of charisma. Her name was Jan Stephenson, and she brought to America more than good looks. Stephenson brought talent, reinforced over the years with sixteen victories on the LPGA Tour, including the 1983 U.S. Women's Open. That triumph, in which she outlasted future Hall of Famers JoAnne Carner and Patty Sheehan, revived memories of the hard work she and her father, Frank, put in together years earlier in Sydney.

I was thirteen. It was the middle of winter, the kind of day best spent snuggled under the blankets, shielded from the cold. Our house didn't have any heat, which made it all the more unbearable. Early that morning, Dad, as cheerful as ever, came into my room. "Why aren't you up?" he asked, sounding a bit agitated that I hadn't yet dressed for our daily practice session. "Dad," I pleaded with

him, "can I just take the bus to school later and be with my friends? It's too cold. I don't want to practice today."

He sat down on the edge of my bed and rubbed my feet. I hoped he would understand and let me off the hook just this one time. Surely, one moment outside would make him realize it was too cold to hit golf balls. After the longest pause, he looked at me and found the right words: "If you get up right now, you might win the U.S. Open one day." I didn't know what he meant, but how could I turn him down after that? If it meant that much to him, I figured I'd better get up and practice.

Dad called me his "dream daughter."

won the LPGA Championship and the Peter Jackson Classic and a number of other tournaments. Needless to say, he didn't know much about being a caddie. I didn't ask for yardage or strategy. Those things didn't matter any-

Almost twenty years later, when I did win the Open, my dad had tears in his eyes. "I don't know if you'll remember this," he started to say, "but—" I immediately interrupted him. I knew what he was going to tell me. "Dad, I'll always remember what you said to me that day I didn't want to practice." Before I won the Open, we had never brought it up.

He was my coach, therapist, best friend, and caddie. He caddied when I

way. What mattered was that he knew the precise encouraging words to say to me on the course, and I was assured that I had someone on my team to give me love and support. In the heat of competition against the best players in the world, you need all the love and support you can get.

HE WAS MY COACH, THERAPIST, BEST FRIEND, AND CADDIE.

I adored my dad. Growing up, I wanted to go everywhere with him.

When I was five, he volunteered as a lifeguard at the beach. I came by and played in the water. I even trained to become an Olympic swimmer, but he figured it wouldn't be a full-time career. It would be over by the time I was fifteen. Besides, the big star in Australia those days was Margaret Court. Dad said to me, "When you grow up, you can be like Margaret Court." I took tennis lessons and showed some promise. Only one problem. I missed my dad. Because he was such an out-standing athlete—he played rugby, cricket, tennis—the government asked him to help build a new golf course. He dropped me off at the tennis courts and went to the course.

What was I to do? Simple. I needed to find a way to get onto that course. My brother came up with the answer. He wanted to go there, too. Not for golf. For snakes. Selling venom was a way to make money for a kid. For

What do you think of that one, Dad?

months, we sneaked over there together after my tennis lessons. I hit some golf balls with a stick while he hunted for snakes.

One day somebody saw me and told my dad, "Your daughter's got a really good swing. You should have her play." He was dumbfounded. "Is this true?" he asked me. "Have you been coming to the course?" I couldn't lie. "I really want to be with you, Dad. I want to play golf." My plea worked. He soon asked for a night shift in his job with the transit department so he would be able to take me to the range before and after school.

From the beginning he believed in me, which in turn helped me believe in myself. Even when things went wrong, his faith in my abilities was not shaken. A lot of times, even as a pro, I cried my eyes out as we left the course because I had played so poorly. I thought it was the end of the world. There was only one place to go to cheer me up—McDonalds. He ate french fries, I drank coffee, and we talked it over. After releasing the anger and frustration, I often went back to the course and practiced. Those sessions turned out to be great therapy. I could say anything to him.

> FROM THE BEGINNING HE BELIEVED IN ME, WHICH IN TURN HELPED ME BELIEVE IN MYSELF. EVEN WHEN THINGS WENT WRONG, HIS FAITH IN MY ABILITIES WAS NOT SHAKEN.

He was extremely sensitive, quite an unusual trait for a man, especially in Australia. My mother told me how our country lost so many women to American GIs during World War II because they acted like gentlemen compared to the overly macho, chauvinistic Australian men. Once, when my dad missed my birthday party, I was so devastated that I went to bed crying. He came home later and stayed up all night to glue together a swan he made from pieces of glass. He then gave it to me when I woke up.

Another time, during a tournament, I was one shot out of the lead with two holes to go. At the seventeenth, a par-five I could reach in two, I hit a good drive and pulled out my five-wood. He couldn't believe it.

"You going to go for it?"

I said, "Dad, it's only 185 to the front."

"Make sure you get over the water," he said.

That warning caused me to use a three-wood

> HE WAS EXTREMELY SENSITIVE, QUITE AN UNUSUAL TRAIT FOR A MAN, ESPECIALLY IN AUSTRALIA.

instead. Bad play. The ball flew over the green into an unplayable lie. I finished with a double bogey and lost the tournament. As it turned out, pars on seventeen and eighteen would have won it. He felt so bad afterward that he sent me a letter: "I owe you ten thousand dollars," or whatever it was [the difference between second and third place].

I've always been like my fellow Australian Greg Norman. I go for it. I can't help it. I guess I became that way because everyone thought I was too small and weak to make it as a professional golfer. I had to prove myself over and over. But Dad once asked me to do him a favor, saying, "If you can't finish twenty-second, finish twenty-third." Before, if I couldn't finish first, I didn't care where I finished. I was wrong. Since then, I've never stopped trying during a tournament.

He always knew how to savor things, which is something I couldn't quite figure out. I was never as satisfied with my accomplishments as I should have been. The perfectionist in me refused to take a break. It wasn't until after he died that I learned this particular lesson. When I won at Saint Croix a few years later, people who knew me well couldn't believe how excited I became. But I had made a promise to my dad and I wasn't going to break it.

When he died in 1988 of prostate cancer, I was devastated. The world seemed empty. I thought

> HE ALWAYS KNEW HOW TO SAVOR THINGS, WHICH IS SOMETHING I COULDN'T QUITE FIGURE OUT. I WAS NEVER AS SATISFIED WITH MY ACCOMPLISHMENTS AS I SHOULD HAVE BEEN. THE PERFECTIONIST IN ME REFUSED TO TAKE A BREAK. IT WASN'T UNTIL AFTER HE DIED THAT I LEARNED THIS PARTICULAR LESSON.

From the beginning Dad believed in me, which in turn helped me believe in myself.

about him constantly. People at tournaments asked me where he was, and I had to explain it again and again. I pulled out of a few tournaments because I was in such pain. My husband was steaming, saying, "Nobody pulls out of tournaments. It looks bad." I didn't care. I needed time to heal. Eventually, my father's death led to the breakup of my marriage. As my therapist said, "Let's face it. Your father was the part of your marriage you never had with your husband." He was sensitive and caring and emotional—all the things my husband was not.

"I don't know if I have ever thanked you for everything," I told him one day at the hospital when I realized he was going to die soon. Before I could keep going, he stopped me: "Please, I want to thank you. You have given me such a fan- tastic life. I always wanted to be a superstar ath- lete and that's what you became. You were my dream daughter." He cried. I cried. My mother cried. A few weeks later, I bought him the first new car he ever drove right out of the lot. He picked out a white Toyota automatic. He was so happy. I'll never forget the look on his face.

PAYNE 21 STEWART

More than any of his wins, which include two majors—the 1989 PGA and the 1991 U.S. Open—Payne Stewart will always be remembered for his wardrobe, a colorful assortment of plus-fours that reflected an elegance long gone in a sport—and a nation. He grew up in America's heartland, Springfield, Missouri, son of Bill Stewart, a furniture salesman whose life on the road he would someday understand all too well. In 1985, Bill Stewart died of cancer. He was only sixty-four. Two years later Payne Stewart donated his winning check from the 1987 Bay Hill Invitational to the Florida Hospital Circle of Friends in his father's honor.

I never met anyone more competitive or more intense than my father. My eighth-grade basketball team was playing on the road in the regional finals. As usual he was sitting in the crowd, letting the official know exactly what he thought of every single call. I guess since he himself had refereed basketball games after graduating from college, he felt he had the authority. No doubt he had the

voice. It was so loud you could hear him from any part of the arena, and he knew it.

Finally, one of the officials, tired of being abused by some obnoxious stranger in the stands—and who could blame him?—called a technical foul. My coach went berserk. "Who is that technical on?" he shouted. "That man up there in the orange sweater," the referee responded. *Thanks a lot, Dad,* I felt like shouting at him. I couldn't hide far enough away on that bench. How could he do that to me? I vowed right there and then that I would never do that to my children.

So much for the innocent vows of youth. I recently did exactly the same thing. I screamed at the umpire during my son's baseball game. As exasperated as the official twenty-five years ago, the umpire turned around and said, "Any more out of you and you're out of here." I laughed, flashing back immediately to eighth grade. Yes, I had become my father. You know what, I'm glad. Because that man, wiser than I ever realized, taught me how to compete and how to care passionately about whatever you're doing, which, in my profession, is absolutely essential.

I certainly brought a lot of passion to the golf

Dad prepared me for everything, except his own death.

> THE UMPIRE TURNED AROUND AND SAID, "ANY MORE OUT OF YOU AND YOU'RE OUT OF HERE." I LAUGHED, FLASHING BACK IMMEDIATELY TO EIGHTH GRADE. YES, I HAD BECOME MY FATHER.

course, probably because my father made me so mad. When I missed a short putt one time, he chuckled and said, "You got your right hand in there." The next hole, when I missed another short one, he started laughing even louder. Nobody got to me like that. Years later, I figured out that he was showing me that the game—and life itself—would always be filled with distractions. You either succumb to them or you survive them. He taught me how to survive them.

THE FIRST TIME HE CAUGHT ME SMOKING WAS AT THE WESTERN AMATEUR. WALKING DOWN THE FIRST HOLE WHILE HE STAYED BACK BY THE TEE, I TOOK A FEW PUFFS, CERTAIN HE COULDN'T SEE ME. HE DID. "HOW LONG YOU BEEN SMOKING?" HE ASKED ME LATER. I WAS SPEECHLESS.

Like any self-respecting teenager, I wasn't about to follow Dad's program all the way. I needed to demonstrate some sign of rebellion. I chose drinking and smoking, the standard vices of my age group. Needless to say, he wasn't too pleased. That was never his lifestyle. The first time he caught me smoking was at the Western Amateur. Walking down the first hole while he stayed back by the tee, I took a few puffs, certain he couldn't see me. He did. "How long you been smoking?" he asked me later. I was speechless. "I thought you were a leader, not a follower," he said. He didn't shout. He didn't threaten. He made his point and then shut up.

On the golf course Dad was more my friend than my instructor. A few years into my marriage, however, he handed my wife a sheet of paper filled with scribbled instructions, such as: "Watch Payne's head. Make sure his left foot is back and his right foot is up. Watch his address. Make sure he finishes high. Watch his speed on putting," and so forth. Soon afterward we found out he had cancer. Did he already know that at the time? Were the notes his parting gift to me? I don't know. I'll never know. I still have the sheet. My wife framed it for me one Christmas.

My dad hated golf carts, so we had plenty of time to talk on the course. One conversation I clearly remember is when I was preparing for my freshman year at SMU. He figured the moment had finally arrived to give me the famous father-son, birds-and-the-bees talk. So what if he was five years late? Maybe he needed the extra time to compose his thoughts.

"Son, don't let girls tell you they're pregnant," he told me. "They do that just to trap you." I laughed. I thought it was funny then and I still do. Yet as a father of two young children, I can now understand the love that was behind what he was trying to say. For that I will always be grateful. I never hesitated to kiss my father on the lips, even in public, and my children and I share the same closeness.

> MY FATHER PROVIDED US WITH EVERYTHING WE NEEDED, BUT THE DOLLAR NEVER BECAME AN ALMIGHTY OBJECT OF ADORATION.

Dad was a terrific golfer in his own right.

I'm so much like him. I am also a traveling salesman of sorts, hopping from one town to another to do my job. I know how painful it is to be away from one's family for a long period of time. That's why I marvel at the way he was able to endure it. He left Monday mornings and returned Thursday evenings,

sometimes Friday evenings, but he always devoted plenty of attention to us when he was home. What I experienced as a child has helped me be more sensitive to how my kids feel when their father is away for weeks at a time.

Money never meant that much to him. That's probably because he didn't have a tremendous amount of it. My father provided us with everything we needed, but the dollar never became an almighty object of adoration, as it is for so many these days. He once looked at the new house I built and said, "Why do you need something like that?" He couldn't understand excess. That was his generation. My generation is different. We swim in excess. But even though I've accumulated many toys—I fly on a private plane, for goodness sake—I think I've always understood, thanks to him, that money is not the answer in life.

Did my dad enjoy his work? I don't know. It's not the kind of question one thinks about as a kid. I hope he did. I know, like many others who grew up in the depression, it was very important to him that his children went to college, and no child of Bill Stewart's was going to drop

How come no plus-fours?

out of college to go to work. He never allowed me to downgrade education. I grew up knowing that if someday I couldn't hit four-irons anymore, at least I would have a college degree to fall back on.

He prepared me for everything. Everything, that is, except his own death. That, he neglected. The one memory that immediately pops out from his fight with cancer is the last day my father and I saw each other. My wife and I had just learned

that she was pregnant with our first child. I was so excited, I couldn't wait to tell him. I also felt that the timing could not have been any better. I was sure it would cheer him up.

He was sleeping in his favorite chair when I walked up to him and whispered: "Dad, I got a secret to tell you. I'm going to be a daddy." His eyes opened up and he smiled. He was going to be a grandfather. I expected him to congratulate me, to express his joy at the moment, to say something poignant, perhaps even to break down. But, I swear to God, the first thing he said was, "Don't buy expensive baby furniture." That was such a typical Dad thing to say.

I probably should have been a little annoyed, but I wasn't. That was his way of expressing love. I gave him a big hug and kiss for the last time. Funny thing is, I never cried at the funeral, which no one could figure out. I'm a very emotional person. I suppose that as the new man of the family, I had to show strength. Six months later I took my baby daughter back home to Springfield. We went to the graveyard and sat down. I finally had my big cry.

My biggest regret is that Dad died before I won most of my championships. He was well long enough to see me compete in only one professional tournament in person, the Quad Cities Open in 1982. I feel tremendously shortchanged. There is nothing I would have liked more than to play with him at the AT&T tournament at Pebble Beach or for him to see me win a major championship.

DAVE STOCKTON

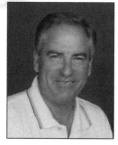

As an only child, Dave Stockton was not ignored. His father constantly took him hunting and fishing, introducing passions that would last a lifetime. Another was golf. Growing up in a house on the grounds of Arrowhead Country Club in San Bernardino, California, the son listened intently as his father, Gail, a former All-American at USC, showed him how to swing, how to stand, and how to think. In 1964 the son turned professional. Stockton went on to win two majors, the 1970 and 1976 PGA Championships. He continues to play a busy schedule on the Senior PGA Tour. The lessons he learned nearly a half-century ago still make a lot of sense.

Don't let anyone out-think you," is what he always told me. For the most part, I haven't. I will not allow myself to get mad like other players and blow three or four shots out of anger, which is really how you lose golf tournaments. You don't lose them with your swing. You lose them in your head. You lose them by not concentrating on every shot, by not having a clear idea of what you're trying to do all the time. These days all the experts say so much of golf is mental. Big surprise. My father knew that fifty years ago.

He was a master motivator with excellent timing, even if I didn't always understand his methods at first. At the 1967 Colonial, I was tied with Tom Weiskopf heading into the

Dad's prime years playing golf were during the depression. His game was tour-caliber, but there was no money to be made in those days.

hooked my drive and never recovered, finishing fourth. But what did that have to do with this situation? Couldn't he have realized I was feeling enough pressure already without bringing up a negative thought right before I teed off?

He had his reasons. He was afraid I was going to hook it badly again and maybe blow this tournament. "Why don't you try to consider hitting a fade out there?" he suggested. A fade? That really wasn't what the hole required, but I listened to him anyway. Thank goodness. The ball didn't fade. It drew like he imagined it might and landed in the middle of the fairway. If I hadn't been trying to do what he told me, I would have hooked it too far left again. I made par and played well the rest of the day. That was my first win on the tour.

My dad rarely came out to watch me play, but that never stopped him from offering the advice I desperately needed. I called him once and said, "Dad, I'm getting the shanks." I

MY DAD RARELY CAME OUT TO WATCH ME PLAY, BUT THAT NEVER STOPPED HIM FROM OFFERING THE ADVICE I DESPERATELY NEEDED.

final round. While walking to the first tee, a dogleg right, Dad suddenly asked me, "Do you remember what you did on the first hole at Greensboro?" Did I? How could I forget? I described, by the ball's flight, what I was doing, and he fixed it right on the phone. I can't over-estimate how valuable those phone calls were in my early years as a professional. In those days it was just me and my wife, Cathy. We left California in February and didn't return until October. I don't know if I would have made it without Dad's guidance. I try to be just as sup-portive with Junior, my son who plays on the reg-ular tour. We talk after every round. I guess we're carrying on a family tradition.

Dad wasn't always so receptive to giving me pointers. When I was a kid, he told me a lot of things I was doing wrong with my swing. He once said, "Your grip is too weak, son. Make it stronger." I had it closed within ten minutes. But when I went back the next day for more tips, he refused to cooperate. That happened on more than one occasion, and it was quite frustrating. It wasn't until many years later that I figured out his psychology. Dad didn't want me to get over-

I can't remember if that one went in.

analytical. He felt I should have fun with the game. He also advised me against reading golf magazines because he thought I should develop my own swing, not copy someone else's.

His knowledge extended far beyond the game of golf. When I was twelve, he said I wouldn't be able to work any longer in the sporting goods store he owned. The next summer I got work at a lumberyard for a guy named Clarence. He was five-foot-ten and weighed about 270 pounds. I'll never forget him as long as I live. He told me to paint six-foot-high fence posts. *No problem,* I thought. *That's easy.* I had painted about twenty of them, when Clarence showed up. I was expecting him to be impressed.

> FOR ALL THAT HARD WORK I MADE ONLY THIRTY-FIVE DOLLARS, WHICH WAS LESS THAN I SHOULD HAVE MADE. I TOOK HOME FIFTY DOLLARS, BUT MY DAD FELT THAT I HAD BEEN OVERPAID, SO HE MADE ME TAKE THE CHECK BACK.

"Son, did it ever dawn on you that some people can see the tops of these things?" Clarence barked. I was speechless. I suddenly realized that I wasn't tall enough to reach the top of the posts, so it took another few hours to finish the job. For all that hard work I made only thirty-five dollars, which was less than I should have made. I took home fifty dollars, but my dad felt that I had been overpaid, so he made me take the check back. Instead of $1.25 an hour, I got paid $1.00 an hour. I truly believe my dad had me look for another job just so I would see the kind of work—and low pay—I might get without a proper education. All his lectures didn't affect me as much as one week with Clarence.

Some lessons, of course, took longer than others to sink in. Much later, after I finished my fourth year at USC and was only seven credits short of graduating, I told my dad I was going to try out for the tour. My game was ready. I didn't need a degree. "No way in the world you're going out there unless you graduate," he said. I went back for one more semester and never regretted it. No matter how I might fare on the golf course, the degree is something that can never be taken away from me.

The same goes for my love of nature, which I picked up from both my parents. We spent so many wonderful times, the three of us, in the mountains or on lakes. Once it snowed at Lake Arrowhead and we couldn't get out of there. We spent the whole day, a school day, fishing and walking through the snow. It was tremendous. My dad and I also went hunting a lot. We discovered so much about each other on those occasions. There really is nothing else to do but share your thoughts and ask questions. We talked about school, golf, and anything and everything that was on our minds. I cherish those moments and have shared similar experiences with my two boys.

Where's the first tee, Dad?

was no money in it. Instead, he became a golf pro until he purchased the sporting goods store. It wasn't a bad life, but it has made me appreciate my good fortune. I just happened to come along at a better time in the game's history than he did. So I try not to get too upset after a bad round. I know how many good players never even had a chance.

I chuckle when I think about him, especially whenever I make a hole in one. Altogether, I've made sixteen, although the first one is the one that stands out. Dad was playing in the group in front of me at Arrowhead when it happened. I aced the fourth hole, which was the designated hole, and I won all these prizes. The kid measuring the shots fell off his stool. Everybody from my dad's group ran over to join in the celebration. They were so excited that the kid had done

I JUST HAPPENED TO COME ALONG AT A BETTER TIME IN THE GAME'S HISTORY THAN HE DID.

My dad was a good player, but he grew up in the depression. With his game, if he had played in the sixties, seventies, or eighties, he would have made it on the tour. But in his day the tour was nothing like it is today. There

it. Everybody, that is, but Dad. He kept on driving his cart, acting oblivious to the whole scene. He never once said "good shot" or "congratulations." A month later Mom aced the same hole. That really irked him. He never got over it. He never made a hole in one.

Dad and me in 1974 at the Pleasant Valley Classic in Massachusetts .

CURTIS 23 STRANGE

In his most precious triumph, Curtis Strange flashed back to his most painful loss. Walking off the eighteenth green at The Country Club in Brookline, seconds after capturing the 1988 U.S. Open in an eighteen-hole play-off with Nick Faldo, Strange broke down on national television, recalling the father who passed away too soon to see the fruits of all their labors together. Strange won another Open in 1989, becoming the first since the great Ben Hogan to successfully defend golf's most cherished prize. His father, Tom, died from lung cancer when Curtis was only fourteen, a rising junior star with so much more to learn.

At that age you think you know a lot about what's going on. But, obviously, you don't. You know very little. You certainly don't know your dad, and it will always cause me a lot of regret to realize that I never will. People come up to me all the time, like Arnold Palmer and Charles Coody, and tell me stories about my dad, who was quite an amateur golfer in his youth. He played against Arnold a few times and competed in six U.S. Opens. He was a very good club pro and was inducted into the Middle Atlantic PGA Hall of Fame and the Virginia State Hall of Fame.

Hearing what he was like is both a pleasant and a painful experience. Pleasant in the sense that it's a chance for me, as an adult, to learn about the man I knew only through the

I never got the chance to properly thank him.

eyes of an adolescent. Painful because it reminds me of what I missed, what so many others my age have enjoyed. My uncle was very close to him, but I never asked him anything. I don't know why. Maybe it's because I've wanted to freeze in my memory what Dad was like when I was a kid. He and I were close, but we weren't buddy-buddy, which I think is the way it should be between father and son. You can't lay down the law when you're best friends. I follow the same approach with my two boys.

I fell in love with golf right from the start. My dad and I spent an endless amount of time dissecting the basics of the swing, trying to understand why certain things went right and why other things went wrong. As a club pro, my dad lived on the golf course. So did I when I was a kid. It was a great place to grow up. You learned etiquette and how to get along with people. During the summer months I left for the course—Bow Creek in Virginia Beach, Virginia—at seven in the morning with him and didn't come home until seven or eight at night. I played and practiced and raked the traps, although I was too young to handle any machinery. I loved it. The game was so much fun and this was where my dad worked.

> HE AND I WERE CLOSE, BUT WE WEREN'T BUDDY-BUDDY, WHICH I THINK IS THE WAY IT SHOULD BE BETWEEN FATHER AND SON. YOU CAN'T LAY DOWN THE LAW WHEN YOU'RE BEST FRIENDS. I FOLLOW THE SAME APPROACH WITH MY TWO BOYS.

One day I went into his office and started crying like a baby. "What's wrong?" he asked. "I can't figure this swing out," I said. I must have been thirteen at the time. I was so upset. He immediately dropped whatever he was doing and we went to the practice tee to work on it. After a few hours he had straightened me out, and I was feeling good about my swing again. That showed me something about how important I was to my dad, because he knew how much the game meant to me.

He didn't tolerate a quitter. We were in the car once when he started telling me how I needed to change my grip. "I can't do that," I said. Boy, did he lose it. "Don't ever say you can't do it," he said. "Don't ever say you can't do anything. Because you can." That is something that has always stuck with me, and you can relate that to

Dad didn't tolerate a quitter.

any aspect of life. I believe anything is possible, and I have passed that on to my own children.

On the other hand, he wasn't too fond of arrogance. When I was thirteen, I played in a tournament where I was beating a few players from our area who were much older than I. Somebody asked my dad how good I could be and he replied, "He has a lot of education ahead of him and a lot of time." That, I realized later, was the appropriate answer. He didn't want me getting a big head, especially at that age. Besides, I already knew he felt there was potential there. I could tell by the intense way he practiced with me.

I never took my father for granted. I appreciated him as much as I could

UNFORTUNATELY, I NEVER GOT THE CHANCE TO PROPERLY THANK MY DAD FOR EVERYTHING HE DID FOR ME.

when he was alive. The real gratitude, however, came later when I became a dad myself. Not having him around when I went through the difficult period of adolescence was hard enough, but not being able to share my feelings and thoughts with him as I became a man was an even greater loss. I'm guessing now, but I think that's when the relationship between a father and son truly blossoms.

Unfortunately, I never got the chance to properly thank my dad for everything he did for me. How does one do that at the age of fourteen anyway? My mom kept my brother and me away from the hospital those last few months, which was probably a good thing. I don't think I would have wanted to remember my dad that way. In the back of my mind, I always thought that if I could win a major champi-

onship, I would dedicate it to him. That's why losing the 1985 Masters hurt so much. More than missing a chance for my first major, it meant I couldn't pay my father back. His biggest dream his whole life was to play well enough in the Open to get an invitation to the Masters. Augusta would have been the perfect place to honor him.

Winning the Open granted me another opportunity. When Rossi [ABC commentator Bob Rosburg] asked me about him after I walked off the green, I opened my heart and I have never regretted it. It allowed me, in some small way, to put him to rest, to complete unfinished business. He never had a chance to share in his son's successes, but somewhere I knew he was listening.

Dad competed in six U.S. Opens.

JIM THORPE

Jim Thorpe grew up in the shadow of his older brother, Chuck, designated by their father to be the star of the family. For years, whatever Jim accomplished, he couldn't measure up, which only drove him to work harder in pursuit of the praise he had long been denied. He eventually earned it, carving out a career—three wins and nearly two million dollars in twenty years on the PGA Tour—that stands among the best ever recorded by a black in his profession. Thorpe looks ahead to the Senior PGA Tour and behind at the past that made it all possible.

Whenever my daddy and I talked about golf, whether it was about Arnold Palmer or Gene Littler, my brother's name always entered the conversation. Mine never did. One night after I shot a 64 or 65 at a minitour event, I rushed home to tell Daddy about it. When I got there, he calmly responded: "Day in and day out, your brother, Chuck, is a better player."

My mother noticed my disappointment and tried to console me, saying, "Your father was only saying that to make you work more." I told myself she was right, if, for no other reason, that I wouldn't feel quite as bad.

I couldn't help but harbor some animosity toward Chuck, who was a much better ball striker than I was. I realized that probably the only way that I could beat him was to put more

131

effort into it. Between facing that challenge and what my dad said, I certainly had plenty of incentive.

Daddy grew up as the son of a sharecropper in North Carolina. When he was old enough to leave home, he took a big chance. A friend asked if he was interested in becoming the greenskeeper at a course they were building in Roxboro. He didn't know anything about growing grass. All he knew was growing tobacco, wheat, and corn. But he decided to try it anyway. In those days you did a lot of stuff by hand. There were no earth movers or tractors. He took the job in the thirties and stayed for forty-seven years.

Daddy developed into a pretty good golfer, or so I've been told. I never actually saw him play a round. Before I was born, he was cutting the fairways one day with one of those antique tractors, when suddenly he heard a big boom. He had forgotten to let the tractor cool off. The explosion

severely damaged his left hand, leaving the pinkie finger and ring finger all balled up. The center finger was crooked, too. After that, for the rest of his life, he could hit balls only with his right hand.

Growing up—I was one of twelve children—a lot of us worked at the course at one time or another. We cut the grass and manicured the sand traps. When we got our work done, he would say, "Get your clubs and go play." Most of the members didn't care, but I remember my daddy telling us the story about the time the president of the club said something to him about it. He didn't back off, adding, "Well, if my boys are good enough to work on this golf course, then they're good enough to play the golf course."

Elbert Thorpe was a man who believed in discipline, although he didn't always take his belt off and beat your butt the moment you did something wrong. He let the whipping build up over a period of time. You might do something on February 1 and he might not whip your butt till

My relationship with Daddy kept getting better as we got older.

February 26, and then he reminded you of all the things you did to deserve it. He had a great memory and he was quite persistent.

Once, when I was fourteen, I took one of his Camel cigarettes out of his pack when there were only two left. For weeks, every night at the dinner table, he said, "Vivian [my mother], I could have sworn I had two cigarettes in that pack." Then he looked right at me and said, "Boy, are you sure you didn't take that cigarette?" I lied every single time. One day, I caddied and made pretty good money, maybe eight or nine dollars, and I had some guy buy me cigarettes. I was too young to buy them myself.

"Here, Dad, here's a whole pack of cigarettes," I told him when he brought it up for the millionth time. Finally, I thought my guilty conscience was in the clear. I was wrong. "Thanks, boy, I really appreciate this," Daddy said, "but you know I really did want that other cigarette, the one that somebody took." The next day my mother urged me to come clean and admit it, "cuz otherwise he'll keep asking every night." So I did. I told him. "Oh, hell, I knew that," he

I REALIZED THAT I COULD DO MORE BY KEEPING A SOUND MIND AND HELPING MY DAUGHTER GET THROUGH THE WHOLE ORDEAL THAN BY TAKING ANY DRASTIC ACTION.

said. "I just wanted you to own up to it."

My daddy believed everyone received his just punishment, if not here on Earth, then with the Man upstairs. I relied on this theory a few years ago when my oldest daughter was assaulted by three guys. My first reaction, as a dad, was to beat the living hell out of them. I was a licensed gun carrier so you can imagine what rushed through my mind. But thinking about what my daddy told me allowed me to stay calm. I realized that I could do more by keeping a sound mind and helping my daughter get through the whole ordeal than by taking any drastic action.

He always told me to be cautious with my money. He was a big fight fan and had sadly watched his heroes such as Joe Louis and Ezzard Charles retire with no money because they didn't have the education to know how to take care of

There was also a lot to learn at home and on the golf course.

it. "Don't blow your money," he said, "cuz there's going to be a time when you really need it. You're not going to be young your whole life."

My daddy handled being black with the same self-restraint. "Son, if you respect them, they'll respect you," he told me. "Play the tournament, change your shoes in the locker room, but don't go ripping and running all over the place putting your nose in where it don't belong." He maintained that the dignity of representing yourself and your race with class speaks louder than anything you might say in direct response to prejudice. Even during the whole controversy at Shoal Creek in Birmingham during the 1990 PGA, I kept my

MY DADDY HANDLED BEING BLACK WITH THE SAME SELF-RESTRAINT.

mouth shut. That's the club which got into trouble for not having any black members. I asked my daddy, "What do you think? Shall I play?" He said, "Just tell the press you are there to play golf and you won't have any problems." He was right. "If we weren't playing for a million dollars," I told the reporters, "then none of us would be here."

The same approach applied to my trip to South Africa in 1979. I went there to play golf during the height of apartheid. That didn't make me very popular with some people back home and over there. At times I even wondered whether it was the right thing to do. Daddy told me, "When you give your speech, don't step on nobody's toes. You can't change their politics."

Daddy and I became closer as I got older, developing a lot of our relationship on the telephone. He wanted to make sure that I didn't repeat some of the mistakes my brother, Chuck, made. For all his promise, he never made it big

on the tour. Chuck didn't put in 100 percent, and he would be the first to tell you that.

I called Daddy every Friday from a tournament site and when I made the cut, he would say, "Well, that's the first step. Tomorrow, you shoot a good round and put yourself into contention, and you never know what will happen on Sunday." Talking to him was very inspirational, quite a contrast with the early days. If I displayed the least dissatisfaction with my play, he'd steer me straight by saying, "Boy, look at it this way, sixty-five or seventy guys missed the cut. You can't be playing that bad. You're competing against the best players in the world out there. Don't get so down on yourself. Just relax and go play."

My mom told me that when I won the 1985 Match Play Championship, "Your dad was glued to the tube all day long, waiting for it to come on. Even when they went to a commercial, he kept

MY MOM TOLD ME THAT WHEN I WON THE 1985 MATCH PLAY CHAMPIONSHIP, "YOUR DAD WAS GLUED TO THE TUBE ALL DAY LONG, WAITING FOR IT TO COME ON. EVEN WHEN THEY WENT TO A COMMERCIAL, HE KEPT LOOKING."

JUST BEFORE HE DIED, WE WENT FOR A WALK. HE SUDDENLY TURNED TO ME AND SAID, "BOY, EVEN THOUGH I'VE PROBABLY NEVER TOLD YOU THIS, I'M MIGHTY PROUD OF YOU."

looking." When I talked to him after the first round of the 1981 U.S. Open, where I had the lead, it was the first time in a long time I had heard such excitement in his voice. He stayed up to watch the late news and couldn't wait to get over to the club to see what the guys had to say.

Just before he died, we went for a walk. He suddenly turned to me and said, "Boy, even though I've probably never told you this, I'm mighty proud of you. You're on the PGA Tour and you've made more money than you've probably ever dreamed of." That meant the world to me. I always believed in my heart that he felt that way, but hearing it from him was what I had been hoping for all those years.

KEN VENTURI

The oppressive heat of that unforgettable June day in 1964 would not deter Ken Venturi. He had an Open to win, a reputation to secure. When a doctor warned him he might not survive if he tried to play his afternoon round—the last thirty-six holes were played on Saturday—at Congressional Country Club, just outside Washington, D.C., Venturi, who trailed by two, accepted the risk. It paid off. He won the nation's championship and its admiration. His resiliency that day was no aberration. Venturi has fought off one adversity after another, strengthened by a role model, his father, Fred, who taught him never to surrender.

As a kid, I stammered all the time. When I was thirteen, a teacher told my mother the problem was incurable, that I would never be able to speak properly as long as I lived. My dad didn't buy it. Instead of showing pity he found a way to make me tough so I wouldn't feel sorry for myself. At the dinner table, if the words took forever to come out, he remained patient, refusing to finish my sentences. My face went into contortions, and yet he showed no anxiety. The point was clear: Learn on your own, son. Life will not always offer you a crutch.

Dad used the same philosophy when it came to golf. I was caddying for him one time at Harding Park, a muni near our home in

San Francisco, when he knocked his four-iron approach into the hole. I jumped up and down, but he didn't believe it had gone in. Finally, sick of my theatrics, he told me, "Go back in the clubhouse until you learn something!" I was furious. "I'm gonna go back in the clubhouse and I'm going to beat you, too." He responded, "Well, I'll wait for that day."

Dad was always there for me.

He knew exactly what he was doing, trying to get me so mad at him that I would work extra hard at the game. Smart guy. I went back to the range and practiced more than ever. It became nothing for me to hit golf balls seven or eight hours a day. That's how I learned the importance of hard work, which is how he

> HE KNEW EXACTLY WHAT HE WAS DOING, TRYING TO GET ME SO MAD AT HIM THAT I WOULD WORK EXTRA HARD AT THE GAME. SMART GUY.

made it in the world. He sold net and twine to fishermen up and down the California coast, working five and a half days a week. He left the house every morning at a quarter to seven and came home at six. Not an easy life.

The biggest thing I wanted when I was a kid was to beat him. That's all I could think about. Although he was probably about a 75 shooter, I knew I could do it. It was only a matter of time. He never did let me beat him, however. One day, a few years later, when I had him four down with four to go, someone came out from the pro shop to get my dad. He had an emergency call. So he laughed, "It doesn't look like you're going to beat me yet."

I took up golf because it was the loneliest sport I could find. It was a secure place far away from everything else, far away from the painful embarrassment I experienced all the time around people when I couldn't talk the way they did. I couldn't say my own name when I was thirteen. It was horrible. I went to Harding where they had practice holes you could reserve for the whole day if you got there first. I hit balls, shagged them, and hit them again.

> I TOOK UP GOLF BECAUSE IT WAS THE LONELIEST SPORT I COULD FIND. IT WAS A SECURE PLACE FAR AWAY FROM EVERYTHING ELSE, FAR AWAY FROM THE PAINFUL EMBARRASSMENT I EXPERIENCED ALL THE TIME AROUND PEOPLE WHEN I COULDN'T TALK THE WAY THEY DID.

I spent hours and hours working at my game.

When I wasn't hitting balls, I taught myself how to speak, using voice changes, echoes in my voice, my hand over my ears—all kinds of techniques they teach today to kids with speech problems. On the tour, people thought I was cocky. That wasn't the truth at all. It was just that when they asked me who was going to win the tournament, I was afraid of embarrassing myself with long sentences I couldn't control. So I said, "Me." Being called cocky was much better than feeling the shame of not being able to communicate.

Sometimes I *was* too cocky and my father didn't put up with it. When I was the number-one amateur in northern California, I told him I was the best player in the world. I could beat anybody—Snead, Hogan . . . anybody. I must have sounded like an idiot. In any case, he stood there patiently, as always, finally asking, "Are you finished, son?"

"Yes, Dad."

Then he told me something that I have never forgotten: "Son, when you're as good as you are, you can tell everybody. When you get really good, they will tell you."

After that, I never told anyone how good I was.

He didn't allow me to make things too easy for myself. At Harding, when it got to the point where I could reach the green from the regular tees, he made me move back a few yards.

"But I can't reach the green from here," I protested.

Too bad. "You'll learn to chip and putt and survive," he said.

As a result, when I was a kid, I could chip and putt with the best of them. Thanks to my dad, when I got on tour I knew how to scramble, and you have to be able to scramble to win.

Manners was another top priority. "Call everyone mister," he said, "until they tell you otherwise." Which is what I did. I earned a lot of respect that way from the older players on the tour. I'm sure that's why I was lucky enough to become friends with some of the greats I had admired, like Sarazen, Jones, Nelson, and Snead. There is no question that my sense of propriety led to Ben Hogan's taking me under his wing for so many years. Hogan, I believe, perceived me as a man of honor and integrity. Knowing him, without a doubt, turned out to be one of the greatest things that ever happened to me in this game.

My dad ingrained in me that one should never break his word. When I was offered a lot of money to sign with an equipment company in the late fifties, despite pressure from the com-

> MANNERS WAS ANOTHER TOP PRIORITY. "CALL EVERYONE MISTER," HE SAID, "UNTIL THEY TELL YOU OTHERWISE." WHICH IS WHAT I DID.

pany president, I held out because I had promised Hogan he would have a chance to match the offer. When I couldn't get Hogan on the phone right away, the president became a little pushy and it looked like the deal might fall apart. But I didn't give in. Hogan didn't try to match it, although he sure appreciated that I kept my word. To me, it will always be worth more than all the money in the world.

Dad also taught me never to give up. "Son, anybody can quit," he said. "That's the easiest thing in the world. It takes no talent." When I was in my slump in the early sixties, caused mostly by neck and back problems, I remembered what he had said. When the doctor at Congressional told me I might die if I tried to play another eighteen holes, I thought back to my dad. No way was I going to stop playing.

My most vivid memory is how my father stood by me during one of the worst moments of my life, when I was about to have my right hand operated on. It was 1970. The doctor told me to "go home and get your stuff in order. You might lose the last three fingers because the atrophy is so bad, and we don't know what gangrene we're going to find in there." I was devastated. "This is scaring me," I told Dad on the way to the San Francisco airport. "I don't know what to do if I can't play golf again." He looked at me and didn't say a word. Then, in the back of the car, as I prepared to leave, he gave me a big hug and kiss and said, "Son, it makes no difference if you ever play golf again."

"How can you say that?" I wanted to know.

"Because you were the best I ever saw."

And away I went. When I got back, the doctor couldn't believe that my mood was so positive. "Doc, my dad told me I was good. Do what you have to do." They built me a new hand and my career was, essentially, over. I couldn't play up to my standards and that's when I took the full-time job with CBS. To this day, because of what my dad said to me, I have not felt sorry for myself. I have not complained about my misfortune or wondered what I might have achieved with a few more years on the tour. I am grateful for what I had.

"You don't have to be better than anyone else," Dad said. "Just be better than you ever thought you could be."

PHOTO CREDITS

Most photos appearing in this book were graciously provided for publication use by the featured golfers, members of their families, or the golfers' agents or agencies. Other photo credits, where known, are: **Page 12** photo of John and Beth Bauer, by Jim Damaske, reprinted, with permission, from the *St. Petersburg Times;* **Page 55** photo of Jack and Charlie Nicklaus reprinted, with permission, from the *Columbus Dispatch;* **Page 57** photo of Jack and Charlie Nicklaus by Toby Massey, *Miami Daily News;* **Page 59** photo of Jack and Charlie Nicklaus reprinted, with permission, from the *Columbus Dispatch;* **Page 69** photo of Arnold Palmer © AP/Wide World Photos; **Page 71** photo of Arnold, Winnie, and Deacon Palmer © AP/Wide World Photos; **Page 76** photo of Calvin Peete © AP/Wide World Photos; **Page 77** photo of Calvin Peete, by Lennox McClendon, © AP/Wide World Photos;

Page 80 photo of Gary Player © AP/Wide World Photos; **Page 84** photo of Jack Nicklaus and Gary and Harry Player © AP/Wide World Photos; **Page 94** photo of Judy and Paul Rankin provided by the St. Louis Mercantile Library; **Page 95** photo of Judy Rankin provided by the Orlando (Fla.) Chamber of Commerce; **Page 128** photo of Curtis Strange, by Bob Galbraith, © AP/Wide World Photos; **Page 129** photo of Curtis Strange, by Ric Feld, © AP/Wide World Photos; **Page 130** photo of Tom Strange provided by Virginia Sports Hall of Fame.

Chapter-opening photos of male golfers were provided by and reprinted with permission of the PGA Tour. Chapter-opening photos of Amy Alcott, Carol Mann, Judy Rankin, and Jan Stephenson were provided by and reprinted with permission of the LPGA. Chapter-opening photo of Beth Bauer provided by Christine Bauer.